THE **CATECHISM** IN A **YEAR**

COMPANION

VOLUME II: DAYS 121–244

Fr. Mike Schmitz

Petroc Willey

Matthew Doeing

ASCENSION

West Chester, PA

Excerpts from the English translation of the *Catechism of the Catholic Church* for use in the United States of America © 1994 United States Catholic Conference, Inc.–Libreria Editrice Vaticana. Used with permission. English translation of the *Catechism of the Catholic Church: Modifications from the Editio Typica* © 1997 United States Conference of Catholic Bishops–Libreria Editrice Vaticana.

Scripture quotations are from the Revised Standard Version of the Bible–Second Catholic Edition (Ignatius Edition) © 2006 National Council of the Churches of Christ in the United States of America. Used by permission. All rights reserved.

Ascension
PO Box 1990
West Chester, PA 19380
1-800-376-0520
ascensionpress.com

Cover design: Teresa Ranck

Printed in the United States of America

24 25 26 27 28 5 4 3 2 1

ISBN 978-1-954882-57-7 (trade book)
ISBN 978-1-954882-59-1 (e-book)

Dedicated to the 2023 listeners of
our **Catechism in a Year**™ podcast
with Fr. Mike Schmitz.

Thank you for being the first group
to journey through the *Catechism of the
Catholic Church* with us. Your thoughts,
questions, and feedback inspired this book.

We are praying for you—please pray for us,
and we cannot wait to see you tomorrow.

CONTENTS

INTRODUCTION

In the first pillar of the *Catechism*, we learned how God reveals himself to us, how God wants us to know him, who God is, how he loves us, and what is true. We also learned who *we* are and what we're made for.

In this second pillar, God reveals how he wants us to *worship* him, how he wants us to *come into contact* with him, and how he wants to *bring us into relationship* with him. God reveals in this second pillar how he wants to be loved and how he wants to love us. And we learn that it is through the sacraments that we get to have a relationship with God.

Essentially, the sacraments bring us into contact with God, allowing us to have a relationship with him. Remember: what Jesus made possible, the Holy Spirit makes actual. This reminds us what the heart of religion actually is.

In almost every religion, there is a creed, a statement of "what we believe." And creeds are important because what we believe is incredibly valuable. But that is not the heart of religion. Each religion also has a morality, or a "how we live." And though that is also highly important, it is not the heart of religion, either—especially not the heart of the Jewish or Christian religions. The heart of virtually every religion is not limited to what is believed, or how individuals are called to live. The heart of religion is *worship*.

Worship is love in action that brings us into contact with God. Until worship happens, the Creed is all theory and the moral life is all acting. But with the sacraments, Christians are able not only to be brought into profound relationship with God but also to sustain and strengthen that relationship. The sacraments allow for that relationship to be healed when it is wounded or broken, and they provide a path for us to live out that relationship.

In every season and in every circumstance of our lives, every moment for the Christian can become an act of sacrifice. Therefore, every moment for the Christian can be an act of worship. The sacraments make this possible. We live out this relationship through the sacraments because they touch all of the big moments of our lives—from birth and life transitions to illness and death, and all of the normal, ordinary moments between.

The sacraments are God's work in our world, and this is something worth reflecting on. When we participate in the sacraments, when we celebrate the sacraments, we're partners in God's work. The sacraments become the People of God doing the work of God in this world in such a way that the Father is glorified and the world is sanctified.

The first pillar revealed how God wants us to know him, and this second pillar reveals how God wants us to live in relationship with him and to love him.

–Fr. Mike Schmitz

Note: This book is based on *The Catechism in a Year (with Fr. Mike Schmitz)* podcast.

HOW TO USE THIS
CATECHISM IN A YEAR COMPANION

This *Catechism in a Year Companion* provides a number of ways to help you live your life in the fullness of the Catholic Faith. In this second volume, you will be guided through days 121–244 of the podcast by three features: ***Reflect on the Faith***, ***Take It to Prayer***, and ***Dive Deeper***.

- **Reflect on the Faith** is a summary of Fr. Mike's commentary on the readings for that day. These are important points to remember and key takeaways as you are learning.

- In **Take It to Prayer**, you will pray along with Fr. Mike every day, using a transcript of the prayer he prays in the podcast. Read it aloud as you listen, repeat it throughout the day, or pray it before you go to sleep.

- Each day, you will be given an opportunity to **Dive Deeper** into the *Catechism*. Sometimes this section will include an image of a key element or event mentioned in the *Catechism* or an answer to a frequently asked question about the readings. Some days, it might be a prayer prompt to use during your prayer time or a challenge to live out what you have heard in your life.

In addition, **introductions** to the four parts of the *Catechism* are included in these *Companions*. Here, Dr. Petroc Willey explains the significance of the part's color coding, notes its key teachings, and presents a breakdown of its sections and chapters. At the end of each *Companion*, Dr. Willey offers a **review**, including a short recap of what has been discussed and review questions to help you recognize how much you learned.

INTRODUCTION TO PART TWO

THE **BREAKDOWN**

This second part of the *Catechism* proclaims how God *communicates his life to us today* and *draws us into his eternal happiness* so that the great sweep of the Father's plan of love, which was laid out in the first part of the *Catechism*, might be accomplished in our lives through the work of Jesus Christ and the Holy Spirit. We will also begin part 3 of the *Catechism* in this *Companion* but will break down its themes in the third volume of the *Catechism in a Year Companion*.

Part 2 is divided into two *sections*. An introduction leads into these, describing the liturgy as our participation in the great work of God for our redemption. It calls the liturgy the "privileged place" for catechesis—in other words, we are being introduced to the *center* of the *Catechism* here. Section 1, "The Sacramental Economy," explains how the sacraments celebrate the Paschal Mystery of Christ and enable us to participate in this mystery through the working of the Holy Spirit. All of the details and elements of the liturgy help us to enter into this mystery. The second section then walks us through each sacrament, helping us to understand how each fits into God's plan and how the sacraments provide the grace we need for our Christian lives.

KEY **TEACHINGS**

This second part of the *Catechism* highlights *God's work* in the liturgy and the sacraments. It helps us to understand how every celebration is the work of God as a *Trinity of Persons*, Father, Son, and Holy Spirit, creating, redeeming, and sanctifying us day by day to bring us to share in his life. The *coherence of God's plan* in Creation and Redemption is brought to light by showing how every element in creation and salvation history is gathered in the sacraments. We see how the sacraments perfectly fit the needs of our nature and equip us for the life of grace so that we become his children, members of the Body of Christ and sharers in the new life of the Spirit.

Reflect on the **Faith**

- The Church's apostolate has one source: Christ, who has been sent by the Father.

- The Church's ultimate identity is fourfold: one, holy, catholic, and apostolic. In our Church, the Kingdom of heaven already exists.

- Whatever Christians do in order to spread the Kingdom of heaven is an apostolate.

- The call of God to every Christian is of its nature a vocation to the apostolate as well. Every single one of us is called, wherever we are planted, to say, "How can I bring the Kingdom of God here?"

- Christ is the source. If we want to bear fruit, then we have to be united with our source, the source of all life: Jesus.

- When we spend time with God's Word in the Bible, or at Mass, or in Adoration, or by learning the *Catechism*, it is all meant to inflame that love, that vital union with Christ.

- That vital relationship with Jesus Christ has to be at the heart of everything that we do.

Take It to **Prayer**

Father in heaven, we first thank you for pouring love into our hearts and your Holy Spirit. We thank you for revealing the depth of your love in Jesus Christ. We ask you to continue to pour that love into our hearts for all the times, Lord God, that we have wasted the love you've given to us. For all the times that we have been numb or indifferent to your gifts. We ask that you please wake us up, help us to acknowledge the fact that you are present, you are God, that you are good, that you love us, and give us that love so that we can be emissaries of love, that we can be apostles of love to your world. God, there are so many people in this world who do not know how much you love them. Help us to be united to the apostolate of the whole Church and to do our small part or our large part to just bring your love to whatever tiny corner of the world we happen to find ourselves. Help us to love the people around us well today. Help them to know that in our loving them, they are reminded of your unstoppable and unfailing love for each one of them. We make this prayer in the mighty name of Jesus Christ, our Lord. Amen.

Dive **Deeper**

THE GREAT COMMISSION

This stained-glass window shows Christ at the Ascension with the Apostles, whom he sent out to preach the Gospel and baptize in the name of the Triune God (see Matthew 28:19). All Christians are called to partake in this mission (see CCC 863).

Reflect on the **Faith**

- Christians are "incorporated in Christ through Baptism"; these are the People of God (CCC 871).

- There are lots of different ministries in the Church, but they all have one mission.

- Christ chose the Apostles and their successors to teach, sanctify, and govern. We as lay people "share in the priestly, prophetical, and kingly office of Christ," too; we have our own work to do (CCC 873).

- The whole body is constituted in such a way that we all need the rest of the body. We all need each other.

- What priests and bishops give to us is something that they could not give on their own—no matter how good or wise or caring or loving they are— but they can give it because of the sacrament of Holy Orders.

- The deepest nature of this ecclesial ministry is service.

- A second characteristic is collegiality—we do not act on our own. We act in communion with one another.

- A local bishop is responsible for his diocese. At the same time, the whole episcopal college is very conscientious about the need for the whole world to be made holy.

Take It to **Prayer**

Jesus Christ, bring us to your Father. You make access to your Father real; you make access to your Father possible. We ask that you please bring us: bring our hearts, bring our minds, bring our lives, bring our bodies, bring our whole entire selves to your Father and to our Father. By the power of the Holy Spirit, Lord God, please accept us, receive us, and let us let you love us. Pour out your Spirit upon us so that we can be more and more like you, Jesus. We make this prayer in your name, Lord Jesus, to the glory of the Father, and the power of the Holy Spirit. Amen.

Dive **Deeper**

God continually invites us to live out the Gospel in our vocation. How has God called you in your role to do his will?

Reflect on the **Faith**

- Christ made his twelve Apostles a "permanent assembly," headed by St. Peter (CCC 880).

- In the same way, St. Peter's successor (the pope) and the Apostles' successors (the bishops) are connected and in union with one another.

- Peter is the "rock" of Christ's Church. Jesus made him the shepherd of the whole flock.

- The Pope is the Vicar of Christ and is the pastor of the whole Catholic Church. He has full power that he is meant to be able to use without hindrance.

- The bishops have this authority, too, but they can only exercise it when the pope agrees.

- In Scripture, whenever someone's name is changed, they are given a new mission. A name is deeply connected to identity, and so it is connected to mission.

- Jesus changes Simon's name to "rock." "And on this rock, I will build my Church" (Matthew 16:18). In Aramaic, the word "rock" is *kepha*, and in Greek, it is *petra*. (See John 1:42.)

- In the Old Testament, the *al habayit* served the king by ruling the house. This was essentially the role of a prime minister.

- Jesus specifically names Peter to be the one who is the *al habayit*, the keeper of the keys, the leader.

- Jesus reaffirms Peter's role after the Resurrection.

- The Latin word *pontifex* refers to a "bridge-builder." The Pope is not the Lord. The Pope is the servant of the servants of God.

- When any one of us is strengthened, we strengthen the whole Church. When we are weak and we choose sin, we are weakening the Church in some mysterious way.

Take It to **Prayer**

Father in heaven, we give you praise and glory. Thank you that, through your Son and by the power of your Holy Spirit, you established your Church. Thank you for selecting Simon, the fisherman, and making him your vicar on earth, making him the al habayit, making him that prime minister, making him the pope. Thank you for giving him that role and for continuing, by the power of your Holy Spirit, down to this day, that visible sign of unity. Thank you so much, Lord. And also, thank you for giving us the Apostles and their successors, our bishops. Right now, Lord God, I want to lift up every individual bishop, that every person who is listening just lift up before you every one of those bishops that are our bishops. We ask that you please continue to guide them, continue to sanctify them, continue to protect them, that they can lead us well, that they can teach us well, that they can sanctify us through their office. Lord God, make them holy. And by doing so, extend that holiness to your people as well. In Jesus' name we pray. Amen.

Dive **Deeper**

Could the pope make a statement against Catholic teaching?

The *Catechism* emphasizes that the Magisterium, the teaching authority of the Church—the pope and the bishops in union with him—is the "servant" of God's Revelation. The Church, then, "teaches only what has been handed on to it" (CCC 86). The pope can provide an authoritative interpretation of divine revelation, exercising his formal authority to teach, either alone or in union with the bishops (see CCC 888–892, 2032–2040). As the *Catechism* explains, the pope is guarded by the gift of "infallibility in virtue of his office, when, as supreme pastor and teacher … he proclaims by a definitive act a doctrine pertaining to faith or morals" (CCC 891). While the pope, as a result of his office, is assisted by the grace of God in all his ministry, not everything he says or writes is guided by the same infallible authority. Some examples include his comments during interviews, remarks on social or political events, or his acts of governing the Church; none of these fall under the charism of infallibility.

Key reading: St. John Paul II, apostolic constitution *Fidei Depositum*, CCC 65–66, 74–95, 171, 888–892, 2032–2040

Reflect on the **Faith**

- Bishops and priests work together in proclaiming the Gospel and making new disciples.

- The pope uses his infallibility when he proclaims a doctrine pertaining to faith or morals.

- The bishops also exercise infallibility, especially during ecumenical councils.

- The successors of the Apostles, in communion with the pope, can propose teachings that lead to a better understanding of Revelation, and faithful Catholics are to obey these teachings.

- Bishops and priests make the Church holy by praying, preaching, and offering the sacraments, as well as by modeling sanctity.

- When the bishops act with authority, it must be in union with the entire Church, led by the pope.

- The bishop should be a good pastor, imitating the Good Shepherd.

- The People of God, members of the Church, possess a supernatural sense of faith and adhere to the teachings of the Magisterium.

- The Church's "Magisterium is linked to the definitive nature of the covenant established by God with his people" (CCC 890).

Take It to **Prayer**

Father in heaven, we give you praise, and we thank you. We thank you for the teaching office, the sanctifying office, and the governing office of our local bishop. We thank you for the teaching, sanctifying, and governing offices of the Holy Father. And we ask you to please help them become the men that you've called them to be. Lord God, you have called them from all eternity to serve. You've called them from all eternity to teach and to sanctify, to govern. You've called them from all eternity to be our pastors, our shepherds, and our spiritual fathers. We ask that you, please, in this moment, in this day, Lord God, give them every grace that they need to be like you. Give them every grace that they need to not break the bruised reed, to not quench the smoldering wick. Give them the grace that they need to teach well and clearly and truthfully, faithfully. Give them the grace that they need to offer the sacrifice of the Mass with purity of heart and with power. Give them the grace to govern and to lead with all humility, but with all wisdom. Lord God, for all those who are carrying a burden today, the burden of teaching, the burden of sanctifying, the burden of governing, we ask that you meet them with your grace. And please bless every person listening to this—that all of us may be led, all of us may receive teaching and be taught well, and all of us may be sanctified because you, Lord God, you are the source of all life. You're the source of holiness. And you, Holy Spirit, are the Sanctifier. So come, Holy Spirit. In Jesus' name we pray. Amen.

Dive **Deeper**

We are encouraged to approach the teachings of the Church with docility. Reflect on times when you may have struggled to accept certain teachings of the Church. How can humility and docility aid us in overcoming such struggles?

Reflect on the **Faith**

- The word *laity* refers to all Catholics other than clergy or religious.

- The call of everyone is to be a saint. There is a "special vocation," then, for lay people "to seek the kingdom of God"—to become a saint—"by engaging in temporal affairs and directing them according to God's will" (CCC 898).

- The role of the laity is to take the grace of the sacraments and the teaching they have received in the Church and bring it into every area of their lives to sanctify the world. Lay Christians participate in politics, the economy, and other areas of society.

- As Pope Pius XII said, lay people are "in the front line of Church life" and should recognize that they are members of the Church and make up the Church, united with the bishops and the pope (quoted in CCC 899).

- We were given a mission when we were baptized and confirmed.

- There are places where priests do not have access. As the saying goes, your life may be the only Bible someone else reads.

- Every aspect of your life can be offered and can become a sacrifice. Every moment in your life can be united to the Eucharist and offered to God.

- Laypeople's lives are meant to be lives of evangelization and mission.

- We can ask God to be present, offer every moment as a sacrifice, and accept whatever comes from each moment. Asking, offering, and accepting can make every moment a moment of grace, trust, and worship.

Take It to **Prayer**

Father, we lift up your voice. We lift up our voice to you. Father, we lift up your name. We praise you right now. We thank you for your Son, Jesus Christ. We thank you for all of our brothers and sisters who have been incorporated into the Body of Christ through Baptism. We thank you for every person who lives out in the world and works out in the world and constantly just brings a little bit more of you into their corner of the world. We thank you. We ask you today, if they're beginning their day as they're hearing these words, we ask that you please help them to bring your grace to their little corner of the world. And Lord God, if they're listening to this in the middle or end of the day, we ask that you please help them to bring your grace to the corner of the world that's their home or their apartment. We ask you to please help all of us. Help all of us bring your Gospel to wherever it is that we live; to bring your light to wherever it is that we live; and to bring you wherever it is that we live. In Jesus' name we pray. Amen.

Dive **Deeper**

Can a lay person baptize in an emergency?

In an emergency (that is, in the case of serious illness or danger of death), the sacrament of Baptism can be validly celebrated by a layperson. As the *Catechism* states, "In case of necessity, anyone, even a non-baptized person, with the required intention, can baptize, by using the Trinitarian baptismal formula. The intention required is to will to do what the Church does when she baptizes" (CCC 1256).

Key reading: CCC 1256, 1312–1314, 1461, 1516, 1576

Reflect on the **Faith**

- Every person is called to be a witness and be involved in the Church's mission.

- Laypeople evangelize through their words and example in everyday life. They can also contribute to teaching the faith.

- Laypeople can and should express opinions in matters concerning the good of the Church.

- Laypeople can participate in Christ's kingly office by practicing self-denial. The laity should rule themselves and conquer sin, acting as virtuous leaders in the Church and human society.

- Laypeople have the power to influence and transform the world's organizations and ways of life.

- The laity's participation in Christ's kingly office extends beyond personal growth.

- Laypeople can have an impact on society through their active engagement and leadership.

- Laypeople should strive for justice and virtue in their efforts to transform the world.

- The laity's participation in Christ's kingly office is essential for building a just and virtuous society.

- Laypeople are called to be agents of positive change in the world.

Take It to **Prayer**

Father in heaven, we give you praise. We thank you so much for bringing us to this day. We ask that you please send your Holy Spirit into our hearts to renew our participation in your priestly office, our participation in your prophetic office, and our participation in your royal office, that we can serve as you serve. That we can serve as servants, as slaves of you, Lord God. That we can speak your Word and speak of you in everything we say and in everything we do. Let nothing we say and nothing we do ever contradict who you are, your goodness, your love, your truth, your justice. And Lord God, help us by your Holy Spirit to offer our lives as a sacrifice along with yours. We are united to you, Lord God. As your Body, we ask that you please send us your Holy Spirit that we can bring your presence into the world in each one of our lives in the small ways we can do, in the large ways that you're calling us to. In Jesus' name we pray. Amen.

Dive **Deeper**

All the baptized faithful are united to the prophetic office of Christ. Have courage to share the Gospel with someone new today.

Reflect on the **Faith**

- Consecrated life involves living the evangelical counsels: poverty, chastity, and obedience.

- Every Christian is called to live poverty, chastity, and obedience in some way.

- Those in consecrated life not only live these virtues but also profess them.

- Consecrated life offers a "'more intimate' consecration, rooted in Baptism and dedicated totally to God" (CCC 916).

- There are various communities that live the consecrated life, some dating back hundreds of years and others more recent.

- The "eremitic life" refers to the call to be apart from the world in seclusion, praying and doing penance.

- Hermits leave the world not out of hatred but because they believe their act of leaving it serves a higher purpose.

- Consecrated virgins and widows commit their lives to poverty, chastity, and obedience. They live the evangelical counsels in their "heart, body, and spirit" (CCC 922).

- Consecrated virgins "are betrothed mystically to Christ ... and are dedicated to the service of the Church" (CCC 923). They may have never been married or may become consecrated virgins after the death of their spouse.

Take It to **Prayer**

Father in heaven, thank you so much. Thank you for the gift of your Church, which has so much variety. Thank you for the gift of your Church that honors the great gift, the great call of marriage and family. We thank you for your Church that honors a great call of chastity for the sake of the kingdom. We thank you for the great gift of your Church that just meets every one of us in whatever state in life we find ourselves. Because you, Lord God, want to meet us in every state in life we find ourselves. Every circumstance we find ourselves, we know that you can find us. And so we ask you right now, for the sake of all religious sisters, all consecrated virgins, right now all widows, right now we ask you for all religious brothers, we ask you to please find them and meet them with your grace today. For all those who have dedicated their lives in this unique profession of the evangelical counsels, we ask that you please give them your Holy Spirit and give them your grace right now, that they can continue to bear witness to you in the world, even if they are separated from the world. And bless all of us, Lord God. Help us to recognize and to regularly pray for these sisters and these brothers of ours. Help them, help us, and be with us this day. In Jesus' name we pray. Amen.

Dive **Deeper**

How is consecrated life different from single life?

Single people "are able to make great contributions toward holiness and apostolic endeavor in the Church" (*Lumen Gentium* 41). St. John Paul II writes, "Christian revelation recognizes two specific ways of realizing the vocation of the human person in its entirety, to love: marriage and virginity or celibacy" (*Familiaris Consortio* 11). Single life, then, is a calling inasmuch as God calls some to live it for a time (e.g., prior to marriage) or even for a lifetime. Consecrated celibacy, however, is a distinct vocation: "The perfection of charity ... entails for those who freely follow the call to consecrated life the obligation of practicing chastity in celibacy for the sake of the Kingdom, poverty and obedience. It is the *profession* of these counsels, within a permanent state of life recognized by the Church, that characterizes the life consecrated to God" (CCC 915).

Key reading: CCC 915

Reflect on the **Faith**

- Religious life is characterized "by its liturgical character, public profession of the evangelical counsels, fraternal life led in common, and witness given to the union of Christ with the Church" (CCC 925).

- Through religious life, "the Church can both show forth Christ and acknowledge herself to be the Savior's bride" (CCC 926).

- Those in religious life all help the bishop minister to the faithful, and their presence is essential for bringing the Church to all people throughout history.

- Secular institutes are communities dedicated to the evangelical counsels: poverty, chastity, and obedience.

- Societies of apostolic life are communities of men or women who do not take vows but who share a way of life in some form and work together for the good of the Church.

- Consecrated individuals dedicate themselves to God's service in very specific ways, such as teaching or reaching out to the poor. They do not take public religious vows, but their first mission is to live out their consecration.

- All of these different paths are ways a person responds to the call of Jesus.

- We all need to recognize that we are consecrated by the Lord. Even those who are not religious sisters or brothers have been consecrated to be in service to God and his Church.

Take It to **Prayer**

Father in heaven, we give you praise and glory. We thank you so much for this day. We thank you for the gift of your life. We thank you for the gift that you've given— placed a call on every one of our lives. That first call that you've placed on our lives is to belong to you, is to be yours, is to be holy, is to let you make us into the saint that you've created and redeemed us to be. Lord God, today we do give you permission. We give you permission to make us into the saint that you've called us to be—first of all, by receiving your love. We give you permission to love us today. We also give you permission, and we ask that you please lead us today. Help us to take the next step, whatever the next step is that you want in our lives. And we ask, Lord, that you please bless all of those people committed to the apostolic life, all the societies of apostolic life. We ask you to please bless all those secular institutions, those people living in the world and serving in the world. We ask you to please bless all those in religious life. Please help them be faithful to their vows. And help them to be united with you, the object of their affection and the lover of their lives. In Jesus' name we pray. Amen.

Dive **Deeper**

ADORATION OF GOD

All the faithful, whether living or deceased, form "one family of God" in Christ (see CCC 959). This artwork by Albrecht Dürer shows countless saints and angels adoring God.

Reflect on the **Faith**

- In the Church, there are "sacred ministers" ("clerics"), the laity, and those living the consecrated life (CCC 934).

- As lay people, we "are called … to be witnesses to Christ in all circumstances" and root out sin through our "self-denial and holiness" (CCC 942–943).

- Through Baptism, all individuals are already children of God, and those who give themselves more closely to serving God benefit the entire Church.

- The Church exists to preach the Gospel and establish Christ's kingship, as Christ commissioned the Apostles and their successors to do.

- Those in the Church are part of the Communion of Saints, which is made up of the living faithful and those who have gone before us, both in Purgatory and in the beatific vision.

- The Communion of Saints surrounds us as a great cloud of witnesses and reminds us of the Church's mission to preach the Gospel and establish Christ's kingship.

- Baptism sets us apart and consecrates us for God's service.

- We can take the opportunity to reconsecrate ourselves and surrender to God's will.

Take It to **Prayer**

Father in heaven, we thank you. We give you praise and glory. Thank you for bringing us here today. We thank you for walking with us every step along the way. We thank you for every person who has been praying for us on this journey. And we ask you to please help us to take one step at a time, help us to hear what it is you want to simply remind us of this day. And help us to not only hear these words, but put them into action; not only to be reminded of who it is you've called us to be and how it is you've called us to live, but truly let our heart, our attitudes, our actions be transformed by this truth, by you, by your grace. We make this prayer in the name of Jesus Christ, our Lord. Amen.

Dive **Deeper**

Each vocation calls us to holiness. Often it can be difficult to understand our vocation in the present moment. Take time to watch the Ascension Presents video on discernment and vocations "What's My Vocation?" (available for free on the Ascension Presents YouTube channel).

Reflect on the **Faith**

- "The communion of saints is the Church," indicating the unity and interconnectedness of all the saints (CCC 946).

- The Eucharist holds a special place in fostering communion, as proclaimed in Eastern liturgies with the phrase "God's holy gifts for God's holy people" (CCC 948).

- God's gifts of communion include spiritual goods, faith, sacraments, charisms, and charity.

- Every member of the faithful is called to be "a steward of the Lord's goods," sharing and aiding those in need (CCC 952).

- The communion of saints promotes solidarity and interconnectedness.

- Even the smallest thing we do out of love benefits the entire communion of saints.

- Each sin hurts all the faithful.

- The Acts of the Apostles highlights how the first Christians "devoted themselves to the apostles' teaching and fellowship, to the breaking of the bread and the prayers" (quoted in CCC 949).

- The communion of saints is nourished by unity in Faith, care for each other, the Eucharist, and prayer.

- The sacraments unite the faithful with one another and with Christ.

- The communion of saints includes the living and the dead, all united in one body.

- We are not alone but are part of the communion of saints.

- The unity and interconnectedness of the faithful extend beyond time and space.

Take It to **Prayer**

Father in heaven, we give you praise and glory. Thank you so much. Thank you for bringing us into your Church. Thank you for giving us communion among all believers, not just here on earth, but those believers in heaven, those who are being purified on their way to you. Lord God, thank you for making us into one Body. You're the gift. You're the source of all life. You're the ultimate destination of all good. Everything we are is meant to be found in you. Everything good in us comes from you. It's all meant to find its ultimate destination in you. So we ask you, God, please, on this day, as we listen to these words, as we pray this reality, help us to say yes to you, help us to say yes to you with everything that we have so that we can, on this planet, be united in love and in faith, be united in your sacraments, be united in caring for one another. Lord God, help us to be united, help us to truly be an image of communion to the world. In Jesus' name we pray. Amen.

Dive **Deeper**

How are we in communion with the saints while we are still on earth?

As the *Catechism* explains, "The ultimate end of the whole divine economy is the entry of God's creatures into the perfect unity of the Blessed Trinity" (CCC 260). The saints have already entered into this divine communion; they enjoy the happiness of eternal life with God in heaven.

We can be in communion with the saints in heaven while we are still on earth because "even now we are called to be a dwelling for the Most Holy Trinity" (CCC 260). We are "created 'in a state of journeying'" (CCC 302) toward this communion, and the more we cooperate with God's grace to come closer to him, the more we are united with those who are already with him in heaven. God wants to save us not just as individuals but as a family, and it is through love for Christ and others that we are drawn more deeply into communion with the saints.

Key reading: CCC 255–260, 954–959

Reflect on the **Faith**

- The communion of saints includes the Church in heaven and the Church on earth.

- The Church consists of those of us on earth, those being purified after death, and those in glory.

- The "union" between those of us who are pilgrims on earth and those who have died is not broken but rather "reinforced by an exchange of spiritual goods" (CCC 955).

- Saints in heaven are "closely united to Christ" and pray for the Church on earth (CCC 956).

- Their intercession helps strengthen the Church's holiness and supports the weak.

- The memory of saints and devotion to them contribute to the strengthening of the Church.

- Praying for the dead is a holy practice, through which we can help them.

- The saints offer the merits they acquired on earth through Jesus Christ, reinforcing their capacity to intercede.

- Saints with larger hearts can contain more of God's glory and offer greater intercession.

- The saints' love for God and others is perfect in heaven, and by their love, our weakness is greatly helped.

- Christian communion among fellow believers brings us closer to Christ, and communion with the saints joins us to Christ.

Take It to **Prayer**

Father in heaven, we give you praise and glory. Thank you so much for this day. We ask you to please, please bless this time. Please unite us more closely to you. You are our head, Jesus Christ. And we exist for you and for the praise of the Father, forever. Give us your Holy Spirit to unite us more closely as one, as one communion of believers, as one body of Christ on this earth. We make this prayer in the mighty name of Jesus Christ, our Lord. Amen.

Dive **Deeper**

The communion of saints can be a difficult teaching to understand for Catholics and non-Catholics alike. Take time to watch the Ascension Presents YouTube video "Do Catholics Worship Saints?" to dive deeper into this beautiful teaching.

Reflect on the **Faith**

- The Church recognizes Mary as the true Mother of God and the mother of all believers.

- Her "role in the Church is inseparable from her union with Christ" and was evident from the moment of the Annunciation to the Crucifixion.

- Mary's faith and union with her son led her to stand by the Cross; she united herself with his sacrifice and thus became the mother of his disciple, John.

- After Christ's ascension, Mary supported the early Church through her prayers and played a significant role in preparing for Pentecost.

- Mary's assumption into heaven shows that she was free from original sin and completely united to Christ; her assumption signifies her partaking in the Resurrection.

- We honor Mary as our "Advocate, Helper, Benefactress, and Mediatrix" (CCC 969).

- As our mother, she continues to bring salvation to all believers.

- Mary's mediation does not take away from Christ's sole mediation. It is similar to how "the priesthood of Christ is shared ... by his ministers and the faithful" (CCC 970).

- Mary continues to intercede for the salvation of souls.

Take It to **Prayer**

Father in heaven, we thank you. Thank you for every person who has been listening to this podcast. We thank you for every person on this journey with us. We thank you for giving us your Son as our Savior, giving us your Holy Spirit as the Sanctifier. And also in that, Lord—in that mission, we thank you for giving us the mother of Jesus to be our mother as well. Help us to be faithful not only to you as our Father. Help us be faithful to the Church as our mother, and help us to be faithful to Mary, our mother in the order of grace. Above all things, Lord, we want to do your will. Keep us close to your heart and never let us be parted from you. In Jesus' name we pray. Amen.

Dive **Deeper**

How can we show non-Catholics that we honor—but do not worship—the Blessed Virgin Mary?

From the Cross, Jesus gave care of his mother Mary into the hands of St. John the Apostle, saying, "Woman, behold, your son" and "Behold, your mother" (John 19:26–27). In this profound act, Jesus made his mother ours as well—the mother of the Church, the mother of all Christians. Therefore, Catholics treat her as such, giving her unique honor and devotion.

We need to point out to non-Catholics that she is the Mother of God, as the Church declared at the Council of Ephesus in AD 431. After this Council, "the cult of the people of God toward Mary wonderfully increased in veneration and love ... according to her own prophetic words: 'All generations shall call me blessed, because He that is mighty hath done great things to me.' This cult ... *differs essentially from the cult of adoration which is offered to the Incarnate Word, as well to the Father and the Holy Spirit*" (*Lumen Gentium* 66; emphasis added). In other words, the honor and devotion we give to Mary is in no way similar to the worship we owe God alone.

Key reading: Second Vatican Council, *Lumen Gentium* 66

Reflect on the **Faith**

- "The Church's devotion to the Blessed Virgin is intrinsic to Christian worship" (CCC 971).

- Honoring Mary is different from the way we adore Jesus and the Trinity, but being devoted to Mary leads us to adore God.

- Liturgical feasts and prayers such as the Rosary show love for Mary and honor her.

- Mary is a sign of the Church's journey toward heaven and its future perfection in heaven.

- Mary, assumed into heaven, participates in Jesus' glorious resurrection and is still a mother to all of us in the Church.

- Devotion to Mary does not replace worship of God but enhances it by deepening love for Christ through recognizing Mary's role.

- Mary's "yes" to God exemplifies the Church's call to be fully conformed to Christ and transformed by his love.

- Mary "is mother wherever ... [Jesus] is Savior and head of the Mystical Body," extending her motherhood to all believers (CCC 973).

- Mary's role as Mother of God and Mother of the Church is a source of hope and inspiration for the faithful.

- Recognizing Mary's unique role in salvation history helps believers understand their own journey and the potential for transformation in Christ.

- Mary's motherhood accompanies and supports the salvific work of Christ, and believers can embrace her as their spiritual mother wherever Jesus is present as Savior.

Take It to **Prayer**

Father in heaven, we give you praise, and we thank you so much. We thank you for giving us your Spirit. We thank you for giving us your Son. Because you so love the world that you gave your only-begotten Son, that all who believe in him would not perish, but would have eternal life. We thank you so much. We thank you for bringing us into your Church. And we ask that you please help us to live in your Church as faithful disciples, as beloved disciples. Help us to constantly say yes to your will, Father. Help us to constantly conform our hearts to yours, Jesus Christ. Help us to always live in the power of the Holy Spirit. And help us always do what Mary did, which is not only point to Jesus, her son, but say yes to the Father's plan. Father, we ask you please help us this day and every day to be your beloved children. In Jesus' name we pray. Amen.

Dive **Deeper**

THE CORONATION OF THE VIRGIN BY DIEGO VELAZQUEZ

The Blessed Virgin Mary, represented here in her heavenly coronation, shows us what awaits the Church in glory (see CCC 972).

Reflect on the **Faith**

- Jesus granted the power to forgive sins to his Apostles through the giving of the Holy Spirit.

- "Baptism is the first and chief sacrament of forgiveness of sins because it unites us with Christ," providing entire forgiveness (CCC 977–978).

- Despite being baptized, we still struggle against the tendency toward sin.

- Through the sacrament of Reconciliation (or Penance), the Church has the power to forgive sins beyond Baptism, offering us hope and forgiveness until the end of our lives.

- The Church can forgive any sin, and all of us can "confidently hope for forgiveness" with true contrition (CCC 982).

- "Christ who died for all men desires that in his Church the gates of forgiveness should always be open to anyone who turns away from sin" (CCC 982).

- The power given to priests for forgiveness surpasses that of angels.

- The Church's forgiveness of sins is essential for eternal life and freedom.

- We should thank God for the gift of forgiveness in the Church and pray for those who feel disqualified from God's love and mercy.

Take It to **Prayer**

Father in heaven, we give you praise. We thank you. We give you glory. We lift up your name. We ask that you please send your Holy Spirit, a Spirit of confidence and of courage, especially in our moments of discouragement. Lord God, send the grace of the conviction that you love us in the midst of our weakness. Especially when we're experiencing despair, temptation toward discouragement, send your Holy Spirit, the fire of your love, to never give up, to never surrender, but always lean in to your mercy, to always lean in to your grace. We thank you for mercy. We thank you for your forgiveness. And today, Lord God, for all the areas that we need mercy, for all the ways that we need your forgiveness today, please meet us in our need. Please grant us your mercy. Grant us your salvation. Grant us your forgiveness. In Jesus' name we pray. Amen.

Dive **Deeper**

Why can the penalty for certain sins only be removed by a bishop?

Jesus brought salvation to the world by taking away our sins through his life, death, and resurrection, to reconcile us with God so that we might come to share in the life of the Blessed Trinity (see 1 John 3:5; 4:10). The plan of God is to save us, not simply as individuals but by making us into his family (see CCC 1). This is why Jesus entrusted Peter and the other Apostles with the power to forgive sins, giving them the authority to act in his name (see John 20:23).

There are three "degrees" to the sacrament of Holy Orders: bishop, priest, and deacon. Bishops enjoy the fullest expression—and authority—conferred by this sacrament. While priests can forgive nearly every sin confessed to them in the sacrament of Reconciliation, certain particularly grave sins bring about an automatic excommunication according to the Church's canon law—abortion is one of them. This excommunication can only be lifted by the local bishop to emphasize the seriousness of the sin.

Key reading: CCC 1, 553, 875, 1443–1445, 1468–1470, 1555–1557

Reflect on the **Faith**

- The resurrection of the flesh means both that the soul is immortal and that the body will be restored.

- "Hope in the bodily resurrection of the dead ... [is] a consequence intrinsic to faith in God as creator of the whole man, soul and body" (CCC 992).

- God slowly made known through revelation that the dead will rise.

- Many Jewish people in the time of Christ, including the Pharisees, looked forward to the resurrection of the dead.

- Jesus affirms faith in the resurrection and identifies himself as "the resurrection and the life" (John 11:25; quoted in CCC 994).

- At the end of time, believers will be raised up by Jesus.

- "Encounters with the risen Christ characterize the Christian hope of resurrection. We shall rise like Christ, with him, and through him" (CCC 995).

- Throughout history, many have rejected the Christian belief that our bodies will be raised.

- The resurrection of the body is often misunderstood, but it is an essential part of God's plan.

- The resurrection is not only spiritual but also involves the restoration of the body to everlasting life.

- Believing in the resurrection of the dead is to live in the hope of God's glorious promise.

Take It to **Prayer**

We talk to you, Father. We beg you. We love you. We praise you. Today, we ask that you please receive our praise. Please receive our thanks. In the name of your Son, Jesus, we ask that you please be glorified, that your name is known, not only around the world by every heart and every mind, but by our hearts and by our minds. Help us to know you better, Father. Help us to love you better. Help us to follow you more closely. Help us to be disciples of your Son, Jesus Christ. And give us your Holy Spirit so that we can experience, in this life, even a shadow of a foretaste of what it will be to walk with you in heaven, forever. Help us to walk with you on this earth right now so that we can walk with you in eternity, forever. We make this prayer in the mighty name of Jesus Christ, our Lord. Amen.

Dive **Deeper**

THE RESURRECTION OF CHRIST

*Christ himself is the resurrection and the life,
and it is only in him that we are raised (see CCC 994).*

Reflect on the **Faith**

- Christ's resurrection serves as an example of how we too will receive our own risen bodies, but they will be transformed into spiritual bodies.

- The way the dead rise is beyond what we can grasp; we need faith in order to accept this truth.

- In the Holy Eucharist, we receive a hint of how our bodies will be transformed, as St. Irenaeus explained.

- The dead will be raised at Christ's second coming, at the end of time.

- Believers have already risen with Christ in a spiritual sense through Baptism.

- Since our bodies will be raised to glory with Christ, we are to show respect for our own bodies and the bodies of others here one earth.

- St. Paul says, "The body [is meant] for the Lord ... Do you not know that your bodies are members of Christ? ... So glorify God in your body" (1 Corinthians 6:13–15, quoted in CCC 1004).

- The transformation of the body in the resurrection remains a mystery, but it is something we as believers eagerly anticipate.

- Every action, no matter how small, can be done for the glory of God, including those performed in our current bodies, which will be transformed in the resurrection.

Take It to **Prayer**

Father in heaven, we pray in the name of your Son, Jesus Christ. We give you thanks. We ask you, by the power of your Holy Spirit, to receive our thanks and praise for all that you have done for us—all that you've done for us in Christ, all you've done for us by the power of your Spirit, all that you have done for us that we don't even know, Lord God. There's so much that we do not know. Not only what you've done for us in the past, but also what you have in store for us in the future. There's so much that we do not know. And so we just give you praise ahead of time. We give you praise for the resurrection of Jesus Christ that you've accomplished already. We give you praise for our future resurrection. We ask you, God, please, help us to live in such a way that we come to the resurrection of glory—that we come to the resurrection of life, and not to the resurrection of judgment. Help us to live in such a way, saying yes to your grace. And for all eternity, we can praise and glorify you; we can love you with everything we are. Help us to begin that today. In Jesus' name we pray. Amen.

Dive **Deeper**

Our belief in the resurrection of the body means that our bodies and souls will be reunited in heaven. What will our resurrected body look like?

God created the human being as a unity of body and soul, and he declared this to be "very good" (see CCC 362–368). The truth of the resurrection of the body is confirmed by the bodily resurrection of Jesus, which shows us that our entire lives matter—how we think, what we believe, and how we act—since our bodies "participate in the dignity of belonging to Christ" (CCC 1004).

Divine revelation does not provide us with any details about what our resurrected bodies will look like in heaven. But we do know that our resurrected state "exceeds" our imagination and understanding (see CCC 1000). Our glorified bodies will be free from illness, weakness, and pain, and they will radiate the light of Christ. As St. Paul tells us, "No eye has seen, nor ear heard, nor the heart of man conceived, what God has prepared for those who love him" (1 Corinthians 2:9).

Key readings: CCC 362–368, 992–1004, 1042–1050

Reflect on the **Faith**

- Death is a necessary transition we must pass through. It is a journey we make alone, even if surrounded by loved ones. "Bodily death is natural," but it is also the consequence of sin (CCC 1006).

- Death brings our life on earth to a close, reminding us of the need to use our time on earth well to reach our purpose.

- Death is the result of sin and is "'the last enemy' … to be conquered" (CCC 1008).

- Jesus died on the Cross in obedience to the will of the Father. Through this act, Jesus "transformed the curse of death into a blessing" (CCC 1009).

- For a Catholic, death signifies union with Christ and the hope of resurrection.

- Preparation for death includes practices like fasting and letting go of attachments.

- Going to sleep in silence is a practice for death, recognizing the inevitability of entering into the silence.

- Christian death is a call from God to be united with him, and death brings us to the One we love.

- Death should be seen not as an enemy but as a means to be reunited with God.

- Longing for God and desiring to see him should accompany the recognition that death is necessary to fulfill this longing.

- Dying in God's grace is essential to see him, and faithfulness is important in preparing for death.

- Despite our shortcomings, God is faithful and welcomes us back when we turn to him.

- Our ultimate goal is to be faithful and prepare for death in order to see God.

Take It to **Prayer**

Father in heaven, in Jesus' name we approach you. In the power of your Holy Spirit that you've poured out upon us, we have been made into your sons and daughters. And our mortal bodies have been transformed. They will be transformed even more fully to be like your immortal body. But right now, we walk amid the thorns and thistles of life. Right now we walk amid the sufferings and sorrows of this world. And right now, we know that we will face death. We will face that moment when we give up our last breath, our heart beats for that last time. And our body and soul will be separated. God, in this moment, prepare our hearts for that. Give us courage in the hour of our death. Send your angels and saints. May Mary pray for us at the hour of our death. And Lord, may you meet us at the hour of our death because, yes, death is the enemy. You did not make death nor do you rejoice in the destruction of the living. But your Son has transformed death and given us new life. And so we ask you, please, at the hour of our death, give us courage. In the hour of our death, give us grace. In the hour of our death, take us to yourself. In Jesus' name we pray. Amen.

Dive **Deeper**

To truly live with Christ, we must first die with him. In what ways have you experienced moments of dying to self? How can you unite yourself to Christ's death in small ways?

Reflect on the **Faith**

- For a follower of Christ who will go home to heaven, "life is changed not ended" by death (CCC 1012).

- With death, a person's journey on earth comes to an end, as well as the opportunity to shape his or her life in accordance with God's will and to choose where he or she will spend eternity.

- The Church urges preparation for death through prayer, asking God's deliverance from hell and seeking the intercession of Mary and St. Joseph.

- St. Francis of Assisi praises God for bodily death, recognizing it as inevitable, but he warns against dying in mortal sin. He emphasizes the blessedness of being in God's grace.

- The Church believes in the resurrection of the body, considering it "the fulfillment of both the creation and the redemption of the flesh" (CCC 1015).

- While death separates the soul and the body, our resurrected bodies will receive unending life from God in the resurrection, as Christ's resurrection guarantees for all believers.

- Original sin introduced physical death, but Jesus willingly died on the Cross to become the victor over death, offering salvation to all humanity.

- Jesus exemplifies mourning as he weeps at the death of Lazarus, demonstrating that even with the knowledge of resurrection, grief can touch one's heart.

- Preparing for a happy death involves reconciliation with God, living a life that praises him, and longing to be received by Jesus at the hour of death.

- Every person decides their ultimate destiny in this earthly life, choosing between heaven and hell, and God's desire is for all to be with him in heaven.

Take It to **Prayer**

Father in heaven, we give you thanks. We praise you. We thank you for giving our life meaning. We thank you for the fact that you see every one of our actions, you know every one of our choices. You know the inner workings of our heart. You have counted every hair on our head because we matter to you in some mysterious and incredible way. We matter to you. And our choices matter. Our choices in this life will echo for all of eternity. And we ask that you please help us to make choices for you today. Help us to not make any choices against you. And if we have fallen, if we have said no to you, we ask you, please, give us the grace. Give us the grace to repent. Give us the grace to say yes to your invitation to let you forgive us. Lord God, give us your mercy and help us to be the kind of people who can walk in your presence, who can live in the light of your face. In Jesus' name we pray. Amen.

Dive **Deeper**

As you reflect on earthly preparation for eternal life, remember that confession is a place of victory! What is your experience with confession? Are there any fears you have that get in the way of going?

Reflect on the **Faith**

- The Church, in the last moments of a Christian's life, offers the sacraments of Reconciliation, Anointing of the Sick, and the Holy Eucharist "with gentle assurance" (CCC 1020).

- "Each man receives his eternal retribution in his immortal soul at the very moment of his death, in a particular judgment that refers his life to Christ" (CCC 1022). This eternal retribution is based on the person's "works and faith" (CCC 1021).

- Heaven is the eternal dwelling for "those who die in God's grace and friendship and are perfectly purified"; there they see God "face to face" (CCC 1023).

- The souls in heaven "see the divine essence with an intuitive vision … without the mediation of any creature" (CCC 1023).

- Jesus died and rose from the dead to allow us to go to heaven. Those in heaven had faith in him and were obedient to him; they share his glory.

- The blessed do God's will in heaven and "reign with Christ" forever (CCC 1029).

- The mystery of heaven and union with God surpasses human comprehension.

- The "contemplation of God in his heavenly glory" is called "the beatific vision," which allows the blessed to see God "as he is" (CCC 1028).

- In heaven, the blessed delight forever in being saved and in being in the company of Christ with all those who do God's will.

- The glory and happiness in heaven include being allowed to see God, sharing in eternal life, and doing "God's will in relation to other men and to all creation" (CCC 1029).

Take It to **Prayer**

Father in heaven, we want to be where you are. We truly want to be where you are. Help us to live in such a way that at the moment of our death, we're able to be where you are. Help us at the moment to live in such a way that we say yes to you with everything we are and everything we have, with our most powerful and free yes that helps us to choose you. Lord God, when we say no to you, help us to turn around. When we say no to you and we choose our own way or we choose the way of the world, we ask you to please pick us up and set us straight. Bring us back to you. Look upon us, and we shall be saved, Lord God. Bring us home. Give us the grace today that if we need to repent and let you forgive us, that we repent and let you forgive us. And if we're saying yes to you, help us to keep saying yes to you. In Jesus' name we pray. Amen.

Dive **Deeper**

A VISION OF HEAVEN

This image of heaven, inspired by Dante's poem Paradiso, prompts us to reflect on the perfect union in heaven among God and his holy ones (see CCC 1024).

Reflect on the **Faith**

- Those "who die in God's grace and friendship, but still imperfectly purified ... undergo purification, so as to achieve the holiness necessary to enter the joy of heaven" (CCC 1030).

- The Church calls this last cleansing Purgatory; this is distinct from the punishment of those in hell.

- The doctrine of Purgatory is based on Scripture references, including praying for the departed.

- The Church remembers the dead with respect and prays for them. The Holy Eucharist is often offered for the departed to ask for their purification.

- Those who sin gravely against God, their neighbor, or themselves and die without repentance are separated from God forever (see CCC 1033).

- The Church teaches that hell exists and that the punishment of hell lasts forever. This punishment entails being separated from God forever.

- The Church's teachings about hell "are a *call to the responsibility* incumbent upon man to make use of his freedom in view of his eternal destiny" and "an urgent *call to conversion*" (CCC 1036).

- The faithful are called to be alert and strive for righteousness to avoid eternal damnation.

- God does not predestine anyone to hell, but choosing to commit a mortal sin and refusing to repent leads to damnation.

- The Church begs God's mercy in the Mass and other prayers, seeking salvation from eternal condemnation.

- The Catholic view emphasizes justification that transforms our hearts. We are called to cooperate with God's grace.

- Purgatory is a process of purification to remove attachments and enable a deep love for God, leading to the beatific vision.

Take It to **Prayer**

Father in heaven, we praise you. We give you glory. We thank you for the grace that you've given us through your Son, Jesus Christ. We thank you for the grace of purification. We thank you for the fact that you give us the opportunity in death even to be purified, the purification you will for us in this life. We ask that you please—for all those who die today—help them to choose you freely. Help them to choose your love freely. Help them to choose your kingdom freely. And help us, Lord God. Like we prayed yesterday, help us now and the hour of our death to choose you by your grace. We ask Our Lady, we ask all the saints and angels, to please pray for us now and at the hour of our death. Amen.

Dive **Deeper**

Why do some go to Purgatory after death? Do prayers from those on earth really help those in Purgatory?

Those who die in a state of sanctifying grace but who have unrepented venial sins or who need to atone for forgiven sins go through the state we call Purgatory. This is a time of purification, a preparation so that a person's soul can reach the holiness that is needed for heaven (see CCC 1030).

As the *Catechism* explains, we pray for the departed because they are members of the communion of saints (see CCC 1055). St. John Chrysostom says, "If Job's sons were purified by their father's sacrifice, why would we doubt that our offerings for the dead bring them some consolation? Let us not hesitate to help those who have died and to offer our prayers for them" (CCC 1032).

Key reading: CCC 1030, 1032

Reflect on the **Faith**

- All those who have died, whether righteous or unrighteous, will rise from the dead before the Last Judgment.

- "Those who have done good, [will come] to the resurrection of life, and those who have done evil, to the resurrection of judgment" (John 5:29, quoted in CCC 1038).

- Jesus will return "in his glory, and all the angels with him. ... Before him will be gathered all the nations, and he will separate them one from another as a shepherd separates the sheep from the goats" (Matthew 25:31–32; quoted in CCC 1038).

- The righteous will receive everlasting life, while the wicked will face everlasting punishment.

- "In the presence of Christ ... each man's relationship with God will be laid bare" (CCC 1039).

- The Final Judgment will reveal the results of the good or evil done by each person in his or her lifetime.

- When Christ comes again in glory, the Final Judgment will happen; only God knows its timing.

- Knowing that the Final Judgment is coming leads us to repent and turn to God with a virtuous fear of the Lord.

- In heaven, everyone will know and be fully known, eliminating pride and shame.

- The Last Judgment encourages care for the poor and needy, as they bring good works before God.

- The Last Judgment will bring understanding of the purpose behind creation and salvation. God's justice and love will prevail.

Take It to **Prayer**

Father in heaven, we give you praise. We thank you for this day. We thank you for giving us time. Now is the day of salvation. Now is the day of repentance. Now is the time for us to come back to you and give you our hearts. We ask you to, please, meet us in the midst of our brokenness. Meet us in the midst of our hesitancy. Meet us in our lives. And we ask you to please give us your grace. Help us to choose you. Help us to turn away from sin and believe in the gospel. Help us to remember that we are dust, and to dust we shall return. Help us to realize and remember that you've made us for eternity. You've made us for yourself. Help us to choose you in such a way that we can spend eternity with you. In Jesus' name we pray. Amen.

Dive **Deeper**

THE LAST JUDGMENT BY MICHELANGELO

This famous art adorns the Sistine Chapel and shows the Last Judgment, when Christ will come in glory to judge the living and the dead (see CCC 1040).

Reflect on the **Faith**

- The new universe is referred to as "new heavens and a new earth," and in it, "God will have his dwelling among men," bringing an end to weeping, suffering, and dying (CCC 1044).

- This renewal will fulfill God's plan for the unity of the human race, and those who have been saved and made one with Christ will form "the holy city" and be "the Bride, the wife of the Lamb" (Revelation 21:2, 9, quoted in CCC 1045).

- In the new universe, there will be the beatific vision of God, providing eternal joy, peace, and unity.

- The world of visible things will be made new for the righteous and will participate in their glory with Christ.

- We should live in a way that leads to living with God forever and enjoying the new heaven and new earth.

- Not only humans but all of creation will be renewed.

- The hope of the new heaven and new earth reminds us that we are made for another world, where everything centers around God. St. Cyril says, "Thanks to his mercy, we too, men that we are, have received the inalienable promise of eternal life" (CCC 1050).

Take It to **Prayer**

Father in heaven, we thank you. We thank you, and we praise your name. We call upon the name of your Son, Jesus, who is the Redeemer of the world. He's the Redeemer of man. Of course, absolutely, Lord God, we say yes to that. He's also the Redeemer of your creation. Lord God, the creation that you made good—that we have broken but you still continue to redeem, and you still continue to use and bring back to yourself—will one day be fully restored. We beg for that day in our lives, in our time. We beg for that day to come soon. Because, Lord God, we find ourselves walking in the midst of pain. We find ourselves walking in the midst of mourning and of grief and of sorrows and of loss and of death. Lord God, until the last day when you restore all things, please meet us in those moments. Please meet us as we walk amid sorrow and grief and sadness and death. Meet us in the midst of those. Because we know that you are the God of the living. You're the God who can bring the dead back to life. You're the God who will wipe away every tear, and you are the God who meets us in our brokenness. You meet us in our broken hearts. And so, until that day, continue to come to us, continue to find us in our brokenness, and continue to redeem it, continue to transform it, and bring us close to you. In Jesus' name we pray. Amen.

Dive **Deeper**

As Catholics, what should we believe about the "Rapture"?

The "Rapture" is a belief of some Protestants about the end times that holds that all true Christians, both dead and living, will be taken up from the earth and transformed into a glorious state. Some Christian groups believe that the "Rapture" will occur before Christ's Second Coming, while others believe it will take place later. The word "rapture" comes from *rapiemur*, the Latin word for "caught up" used in 1 Thessalonians 4:17 in the Vulgate version of the Bible.

The Church affirms that Christ will return at the end of time in his Second Coming and that all people, living and dead, will be raised and will be judged in the Final Judgement. The Church does not accept the idea that Christians will be taken up from the earth prior to this glorious event. In fact, belief in the Rapture dates only from the 1830s, and most Protestant and Eastern Orthodox Christians reject it.

Reflect on the **Faith**

- The blessed in heaven form the Church there, beholding God face-to-face.

- Anyone who is in the state of grace at the time of death but who is in need of purification goes to Purgatory to attain the sanctity that is needed for heaven. The Church prays for the departed, offering the holy Mass in particular, to beg God's mercy for them.

- "The Church warns the faithful of the 'sad and lamentable reality of eternal death,'" or hell, which is separation from God forever (CCC 1056).

- The Church prays for the salvation of all and acknowledges "that God 'desires all men to be saved'" (CCC 1058).

- "On the Day of Judgment all men will appear in their own bodies before Christ's tribunal to render an account of their own deeds" (CCC 1059).

- "At the end of time, the Kingdom of God will come in its fullness. Then the just will reign with Christ for ever, glorified in body and soul" (CCC 1060).

- The last word of the Creed, like the last word of the Bible, is "Amen." This indicates our reliance on God and also his fidelity.

- It is important to contemplate our death and the moment after, envisioning the gaze of God upon us with either joy or sorrow.

- Praying for the grace of final perseverance and a happy death is essential, trusting in God's faithfulness and seeking his grace.

Take It to **Prayer**

Father in heaven, we thank you so much. We give you praise and glory. Thank you for bringing us here to this day. Thank you for bringing us here to this moment. Thank you for bringing us here all the way through pillar one. We ask that you, please, as we prepare ourselves for our death, as we prepare ourselves to give you our ultimate and final amen—that we trust in your amen, your amen of faithfulness, our amen of belief but your amen of faithfulness; that we can trust who you are because you are the God of the amen. You are the God of truth. You are the God who is faithful. And so as we once again reflect on these nuggets of what it is to die in you, Jesus Christ, we ask that you please come and meet us because you, Christ, are the Father's definitive amen. You're the Father's definitive Word. You're the Father's definitive Truth. Help us to give our amen to you. In Jesus' name we pray. Amen.

Dive **Deeper**

"Amen" is often a word we say without thinking about its true meaning. Find time today to truly pray the word "amen" and become more aware of its power.

Reflect on the **Faith**

- Today Bishop Cozzens joins us to introduce part 2.

- The number of Catholics attending Sunday Mass has dropped, according to a post-COVID study.[1] This means that many people have not had an encounter with Jesus in the Eucharist.

- Pillar two of the *Catechism* concerns liturgy and the sacraments. This is how the Church prays. But it is more than how the Church prays; it is how the Church continues her life throughout time.

- The liturgy and sacraments transform us.

- The liturgy is Jesus' own perfect worship. It is his prayer that he made to the Father in his gift of self on the Cross.

- In the liturgy, we are participating in Christ's prayer.

- The signs and symbols of the liturgy show that it is trying to draw us in to heaven, where Jesus has gone ahead.

- When we celebrate the sacraments, we are not just praying our own prayer, we are praying the prayer of Jesus himself.

- The liturgy is the official prayer of the Church.

- The Holy Mass and the Eucharist are the center of all liturgies and the center of our whole liturgical life.

- The Church also has the Liturgy of the Hours that priests and religious and some laypeople pray every day.

- The liturgy is a way that individual members of the Church can enter into the overall prayer of the Church.

- The sacraments provide a direct encounter with God.

- God reveals himself to us so we can participate in his life (see CCC 1).

Take It to **Prayer**

Father in heaven, we give you praise and glory. Thank you for bringing us to the second pillar of the Catechism. Thank you for bringing us to this place where we can learn more about you, where we can know your identity and know our deepest identity as your beloved creation, as those who have been adopted by you in Baptism and made into your sons and your daughters. Help us to know you as our Father. Help us to know you, God, as Father, Son, and Holy Spirit and be drawn into your love. This day, we ask you to please bless this conversation. Bless Bishop Cozzens, bless me, and please bless everyone who is listening to us today. In Jesus' name we pray. Amen.

Dive **Deeper**

The Eucharist is a life-changing encounter with Jesus. Learn more about it by watching the Ascension Presents YouTube video called "How the Eucharist Changed My Life."

Reflect on the **Faith**

- The liturgy is a celebration of the Christian mystery and the sacramental economy. It focuses on the Paschal Mystery of Christ, which brought about our salvation.

- Liturgy is "an exercise of the priestly office of Jesus Christ" and "every liturgical celebration, because it is an action of Christ the priest and of his Body which is the Church, is a sacred action" (CCC 1070).

- Liturgy "makes the Church present and manifests her as the visible sign of the communion in Christ between God and men" (CCC 1071).

- Liturgy is "a participation in Christ's own prayer addressed to the Father in the Holy Spirit. In the liturgy, all Christian prayer finds its source and goal" (CCC 1073).

- The liturgy is "the privileged place for catechizing the People of God," and "liturgical catechesis aims to initiate people into the mystery of Christ" (CCC 1074–1075).

- The goal of liturgical catechesis is to help people understand the signs that are used in the liturgy and to experience the sacred realities to which they refer.

- "The liturgy is the summit toward which the activity of the Church is directed; it is also the font from which all her power flows" (CCC 1074).

Take It to **Prayer**

Father in heaven, we give you thanks. We praise you. We give you glory, and we love you. Help us to love you not just in our hearts, not just to love you in our thoughts or having a good attitude or a good opinion of you, Lord God, but help us to love you through worship. Help us to love you by participating in your work, your work of sanctifying this world, your work of redeeming this world, your work of transforming this world, your work of reaching out to our brothers and sisters who are in the most need. We ask you to please help us to do that now in the course of our lives. In Jesus' name we pray. Amen.

Dive **Deeper**

Consider the significance of the liturgy that takes place at each Mass. How does our participation invite us more closely into a relationship with Christ? Take time today to reflect on what it means to participate fully in the liturgy.

Reflect on the **Faith**

- "The Church was made manifest to the world" when the Holy Spirit came at Pentecost, beginning a "new era" called "the age of the Church" (CCC 1076).

- In this age, "Christ manifests, makes present, and communicates his work of salvation through the liturgy of his Church" (CCC 1076).

- "Blessing is a divine and life-giving action," originating from God the Father. "When applied to man, the word 'blessing' means adoration and surrender to his Creator in thanksgiving" (CCC 1078).

- The Father blesses us through his Word, particularly through the gift of the Holy Spirit.

- The liturgy involves both blessing God and coming before the Father with "the offering his own gifts" and seeking the outpouring of the Holy Spirit (CCC 1083).

- The sacramental economy is recognized in both the Eastern and Western traditions of the Church. We see the many liturgical expressions and rites within the Catholic Church.

- What a gift it is to be able to live in the age of the Church where Jesus continues to come to us to sanctify, redeem, heal, and forgive us as he feeds us through his sacraments.

Take It to **Prayer**

Father in heaven, we thank you. We give you praise and glory. We thank you and praise your name. We bless your name, Lord God. We bless your name, and we surrender and adore you in thanksgiving. That is our blessing. Our blessing is a prayer of adoration and a prayer of surrender to you in thanksgiving. So we thank you. We ask you to please hear our prayer. Receive the blessing that we offer you as little as we are, broken as we are, and good as you are. Lord God, receive our blessing. Receive our adoration. Receive our surrender to you in thanksgiving. We make this prayer in the mighty name of Jesus Christ, our Lord. Amen.

Dive **Deeper**

God the Father has given us the liturgy as his greatest gift. Do you view God as a loving Father who wishes to give freely? Have you pondered how God is continually blessing you at each Mass?

Reflect on the **Faith**

- "Sacraments are perceptible signs (words and actions) accessible to our human nature. By the action of Christ and the power of the Holy Spirit they make present efficaciously the grace that they signify" (CCC 1084).

- The Paschal Mystery of Christ, unlike other events in history, "transcends all times while being made present in them all" (CCC 1085).

- In order to bring us what he has done for us, Jesus gave the Apostles not just the ability of preaching but the "power of sanctifying" (CCC 1087).

- In John 20, we read that Jesus, who has risen from the dead, says to the disciples, "'Peace be with you. As the Father has sent me, even so I send you.' And when he had said this, he breathed on them, and said to them, 'Receive the Holy Spirit. If you forgive the sins of any, they are forgiven; if you retain the sins of any, they are retained'" (John 20:21–23).

- "Christ is always present in his Church, especially in her liturgical celebrations" (CCC 1088).

- In the liturgy, the Father is given glory and the People of God are made holy.

- Through the liturgy, we join Jesus Christ and the saints in glorifying the Lord and looking forward to his Second Coming.

Take It to **Prayer**

Father in heaven, thank you so much. Thank you for the gift of the fact that what Jesus had done for us, what he has done for us two thousand years ago halfway around the world for many of us, comes to us now. It comes to us here in our little towns, in our big cities, in our small parishes, in our giant churches. Lord God, what your Son has done for us, we have access to. We have access to you, and you make yourself present. You make the Holy Trinity present at every single liturgy, Lord God. You make yourself completely accessible to us because you are good and you love us, and we thank you. We thank you for everything you've done. We thank you for the Paschal Mystery, the life, death, and resurrection of Jesus, which comes to us in every liturgy, especially in the Liturgy of the Eucharist. We thank you, Lord God. Please, help us to have eyes that see right, to help us look, Father. To have eyes that recognize your presence, your work, your Son, your Holy Spirit in the liturgy, especially when our eyes can be so obscured by just seeing ordinary things. But Lord God, you use ordinary things in an extraordinary way. You use ordinary things to give us extraordinary grace. You use ordinary things to give us yourself. And so help us have eyes to see and a faith that receives and worships and loves you. In Jesus' name we pray. Amen.

Dive **Deeper**

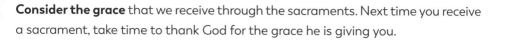

Consider the grace that we receive through the sacraments. Next time you receive a sacrament, take time to thank God for the grace he is giving you.

Reflect on the **Faith**

- Because of the sacraments, we are as close to the Lord Jesus as believers were at any other time in salvation history.

- When we receive the sacraments, the Holy Spirit prepares our hearts and helps us respond with faith.

- Many things that we do in the liturgy have their roots in Scripture. The Christian liturgy is the fulfillment of everything that was laid down by the Law of Moses. The Jewish way of worship is fulfilled in Jesus.

- Within the Church, the Holy Spirit enables believers to "live from the life of the risen Christ" (CCC 1091). That is what we are made for.

- The sacraments are not magic. They happen in cooperation with us.

- If we receive Holy Communion every single day but we do not cooperate and shape our wills to the Father's will, we will be unchanged.

- We are never meant to show up to the sacraments and leave the exact same way that we arrived; we are meant to be changed.

- Because we have been brought into the Body of Christ by the Holy Spirit, who unites us, the most important thing about you and about me is that each of us is a son or a daughter of God.

Take It to **Prayer**

Father in heaven, we praise you and give you glory. We thank you for this day. We thank you for your Holy Spirit that has brought us to this day. We know, Lord God, that if left to ourselves, we would not choose to be here. We would not choose to press play. Left to ourselves, Lord God, we would go our own way. But we are not left to ourselves. You have not left us to ourselves. You have lifted us up out of ourselves, to draw us close to you. And so, please, help us to say yes to your Holy Spirit, help us to say yes to your will in this moment and in every moment of this day and for the rest of our lives so that we can spend eternity with you. In Jesus' name we pray. Amen.

Dive **Deeper**

THE HOLY SPIRIT

The Holy Spirit appears in the form of a dove at Jesus' baptism. The dove's depiction here reminds us of the Spirit's role in preparing us to receive Christ and his grace (see CCC 1092).

Reflect on the **Faith**

- The Scriptural concept of a memorial, described by the Greek word *anamnesis*, is a remembrance that is unique. It not just remembering a past event but bringing it to the here and now.

- The Holy Spirit is the one who inspired the Word of God. Sacred Scripture is not only proclaimed in the Mass but also explained in the Mass.

- Christ and his salvific work are made present by the Holy Spirit in the Church's liturgy.

- The liturgy, especially the Eucharist, "is the *memorial* of the mystery of salvation" (CCC 1099).

- "The word of God is living and active, sharper than any two-edged sword" (Hebrews 4:12), but sometimes we are indifferent. We need the Holy Spirit to help us, because we don't even know how to hear God's Word as we ought to.

- The prophet Samuel was called by God and said, "Speak, LORD, for your servant hears" (1 Samuel 3:9). We are called to have that kind of open disposition.

- My invitation for all of us whenever we approach the Scriptures is to respond. We respond with receptivity, saying, "Speak, Lord. Your servant is listening." We respond with agreement, saying, "Amen." And we respond with readiness to do what the Lord is calling us to do.

- *Anamnesis*, the remembrance in the liturgy, brings past events into the present reality for the community.

Take It to **Prayer**

Father in heaven, we trust you. We love you, and we dedicate this day to you. Whether this is the beginning of the day for us, the middle of the day for us, or the very end of the day, this day is yours. And by the power of your Holy Spirit, we ask that you please help us to remember, to never forget all that you've done for us, not only in the past through your Son, Jesus Christ, but also what you've done for us yesterday, in that past, the recent past—what you've done for us at these beats and moments in our own life history—what you're doing for us right now. Help us to never, ever forget. Help us to always remember that you are present, that you are here, and your Holy Spirit makes present and actual what your Son, Jesus Christ our Lord, made possible. We make this prayer in the mighty name of that same Lord and Savior, Jesus Christ, as we pray. Amen.

Dive **Deeper**

The Holy Spirit is continually inviting us to go deeper into the mystery of salvation. Spend time in prayer asking the Holy Spirit to grant you his fruits and strengthen his gifts.

Reflect on the **Faith**

- The Holy Spirit brings the events of Christ's salvation into the present in the liturgy.

- The liturgy celebrates the Paschal mystery of Christ, and each celebration involves the coming of the Holy Spirit.

- In the *Epiclesis*, the priest prays that God the Father give the Holy Spirit to transform the bread and wine into the Body, Blood, Soul, and Divinity of Christ.

- The liturgy is the close working together of the Holy Spirit and the Church, leading to being united to God and united to fellow Christians.

- The Church prays that the Holy Spirit change our hearts to be like Christ, guide us to preserve the oneness of the Church, and help us to act with charity.

- "In the liturgy of the Church, God the Father is blessed and adored," who has bestowed "the Spirit of filial adoption" (CCC 1110).

- "Christ's work in the liturgy is sacramental: ... his mystery of salvation is made present there by the power of his Holy Spirit" (CCC 1111).

- The Mass makes the events of salvation present, regardless of the external elements, and invites believers to participate in the mysteries.

Take It to **Prayer**

Father in heaven, we praise your name, and we give you glory. We thank you so much for the gift of your Son. We thank you for the gift of your love for us. We thank you for the love between you and the Son that is the Holy Spirit that has been poured out into our hearts. In this moment, Lord God, we ask you to come and make your saving work present in our lives, now—in the liturgy, outside the liturgy, in our lives, Lord God. By the power of your Holy Spirit, make present the reality of the Son's life, death, and resurrection. In everything that we do, let every part of our lives be conformed to you. Let every part of our lives be touched and transformed by you. We make this prayer in the mighty name of Jesus Christ, our Lord. Amen.

Dive **Deeper**

For many, the Eucharist can be the most beautiful and daunting teaching we have. Dive deeper into this teaching with the Ascension Presents YouTube video "The Shocking Reality of the Eucharist."

Reflect on the **Faith**

- When we participate in the sacraments, we are not just remembering.

- The sacraments "are actions of the Holy Spirit at work in his Body, the Church" (CCC 1116).

- The Church, led by the Holy Spirit, has come to perceive the seven sacraments.

- Those who have been baptized have been anointed to share in Christ's priesthood, his mission of prophecy, and his kingship. They have a baptismal priesthood, or kingdom priesthood.

- Priests are servant leaders. Every father is the servant of his family, and priests are meant to be the same—to lay down their lives for and serve all those in the baptismal priesthood.

- "The ordained priesthood guarantees that it really is Christ who acts in the sacraments through the Holy Spirit for the Church" (CCC 1120).

- Jesus commissioned the Apostles. In the Gospel, we read that he said, "As the Father has sent me, even so I send you" (John 20:21).

- The sacraments are given to us by Jesus and come to us by the power of the Holy Spirit through the ministry of the ordained priesthood. All of the faithful participate in them in their baptismal priesthood.

Take It to **Prayer**

Father in heaven, you're good. You're God. We love you. And we ask you to please send your Holy Spirit to be with us in this moment. And we know that we have access to your fatherly heart by the work of your Son, Jesus; by the gift of your Holy Spirit; and by the fact that you have called us and made us into your sons and daughters through Baptism. Lord, you continue to pour out your Holy Spirit upon us. And we ask that you, in this moment, come to us in our weakness. Come to us in our need. Come to us in our brokenness and give us healing. Come to us in our frustration and give us peace. Come to us in our weakness and give us strength. Come to us in our fear and give us courage. Lord God, we do not ask for you to make this world safer. We do ask you to help us be more brave, to be more courageous, and to be strong. Help us to love you the way you love us. In Jesus' name we pray. Amen.

Dive **Deeper**

The seven sacraments manifest the love of God for man. Reflect on how the sacraments offer us a tangible experience of God's love and grace. How can we approach the sacraments with a deeper sense of reverence and awe, recognizing their transformative power in our lives?

Reflect on the **Faith**

- The sacraments are not empty rites and rituals. They exist to make us holy; through them, the Church is strengthened and God is worshipped. This is what the sacraments are for and what they do.

- Evangelization is the proclaiming of the Good News. In the Great Commission at the end of Matthew's Gospel, Jesus sent out the disciples to spread that Good News.

- In the Great Commission, Jesus connects the call to evangelize with the call to baptize. Evangelizing involves offering the sacraments.

- At every Mass, God is glorified for the good of all the Church.

- It is so important that we do not stay away from the sacraments when we are struggling but that we enter into them.

- In the principle *lex orandi, lex credendi* (the law of praying, the law of believing), we claim that "the Church believes as she prays" (CCC 1124).

- The *Catechism* states, "No sacramental rite may be modified or manipulated at the will of the minister or the community" (CCC 1125). For example, in the West, the Roman Missal presents how the Liturgy of the Eucharist is to be celebrated.

- We cannot change something in how we pray without, possibly, expressing a change in belief. Not even the Pope can alter the liturgy "arbitrarily" (CCC 1125).

- Every time we approach any of the sacraments, God is glorified. Whether we feel it or not, any time we use the gifts of our Father, he is glorified.

Take It to **Prayer**

Father in heaven, we give you praise and glory. We thank you. We ask that you, please, help us to participate in the sacraments in such a way that, yes, this world is sanctified; that we are sanctified; that your Church, the Body of Christ, is built up and strengthened and mobilized. We also pray that you may be glorified above all. In everything, Father, may you be known. May you be loved. May you be worshipped. May we give our hearts to you the way you have given your heart to us. Help us love you the way you love us. Help us love each other the way you've called us to. And help us to be yours. Help us to respond and walk in faith. Help us to do this in every moment of our lives. And, particularly, help us to do this when we encounter you in your sacraments. In Jesus' name we pray. Amen.

Dive **Deeper**

THE ROMAN MISSAL

In the Church's liturgy, especially in the sacramental mysteries, the Church acknowledges the apostolic faith and calls us to embrace it with love (CCC 1124).

Reflect on the **Faith**

- Sacraments are "*efficacious*," not just symbols (CCC 1127). A sacrament is a sacred sign that causes what it symbolizes.

- Baptism is a sign of birth, and it actually does make us into God's sons and daughters. The sacrament of Reconciliation is a sign of God's forgiveness, and it actually does forgive our sins. The sacrament of the Eucharist is the sign of Christ's Body and Blood, and it actually is Christ's Body and Blood.

- The sacrament happens every single time, but whether or not we experience the effects of the sacrament will be based on our openness to receive it.

- Sacraments "are *necessary for salvation*" (CCC 1129). Jesus, our Lord and Savior, said this, and the Church declares it.

- In chapter 3 of the Gospel of John, Jesus says, "Unless one is born of water and the Spirit, he cannot enter the kingdom of God" (John 3:5). So Baptism is necessary.

- In chapter 6 of the Gospel of John, Jesus says, "Unless you eat the flesh of the Son of man and drink his blood, you have no life in you" (John 6:52). So the Eucharist is necessary for salvation.

- Through the sacraments, the Spirit of the Father says to each of us, "You are my child."

- Because of what Jesus Christ has done for us and the power of the Holy Spirit abiding in us, we become temples of the Holy Spirit.

- We now are sharers in the life of God. If you have been baptized, you share in the very nature of God.

Take It to **Prayer**

Father in heaven, you are good, and all your works are good. You lead us to your heart. You share with us your Holy Spirit. You give us your Son to be our Lord, to be our Savior, to be our brother. Lord God, you even call us your friends. Help us. Help us to allow you to be Lord. Help us to trust you to be our Savior. Help us to walk with you as our brother. And help us to be vulnerable enough to be your friend. Help us to be your faithful friend. We make this prayer in the mighty name of Jesus Christ, our Lord. Amen.

Dive **Deeper**

What does it mean that "there is no salvation outside the Church"?

The name Jesus means "God saves." So Jesus' name describes "both his identity and his mission" (CCC 430). His work of salvation is the very center of the Catholic Faith. It is no accident that the *Catechism* references 1 Timothy 2:3–4 repeatedly: "God our Savior ... desires all men to be saved and to come to the knowledge of the truth." In its prologue, the *Catechism* quotes from Scripture in reference to Christ: "There is no other name under heaven given among men by which we must be saved" (Acts 4:12). There is only one Savior, Jesus.

To make his salvation available to all, Jesus established the Catholic Church. The name *catholic* refers to the universality of the Church in two ways: (1) the Church has been entrusted by Jesus with "the fullness of the means of salvation"—the true faith, the sacraments, and the authority to teach and govern granted to the Apostles and their successors, the bishops; and (2) the Church's ministry is for all humanity, since everyone is called to salvation in Christ (see CCC 830–831). The phrase "outside the Church there is no salvation" means that *all* of God's saving work in the world flows through Christ and his Church. The *Catechism* emphasizes, over and over again, the urgent call to holiness, prayer, and mission. The Church is like Noah's ark, a place of refuge and salvation from the Flood, and is impelled by the love of Christ to seek to help every person to enter.

Key reading: CCC 830–856

Reflect on the **Faith**

- The sacraments bring heaven to earth right now, but they also are fulfilled in the kingdom of God, in eternity. The sacraments are where time and eternity touch.

- Right now, we participate in that grace. In every sacrament, we share in what Jesus Christ has established and won for us.

- The sacraments mediate the grace of our Lord Jesus Christ to us. The day will come in heaven when there is no mediation and we see the Lord as he is face-to-face. But right now, he comes to us through signs, through sacraments.

- The priest says the same words of absolution every time in confession. But it is not an empty ritual. It is an "efficacious" ritual that "make[s] present the graces" Jesus has won for us on the Cross—forgiveness, mercy, and reconciliation with God himself (CCC 1130).

- St. Thomas Aquinas says that a sacrament "prefigures what that Passion pledges to us—future glory" (CCC 1130).

- If we have been baptized, we have been brought into a share in Christ's priesthood—given a share of the ability to offer up the great sacrifice to the Father in the power of the Holy Spirit.

- We are not learning simply about something that someone else does. We are also learning about how we are being called to enter into this, into full and active participation in the liturgy.

- Many Catholics know that Jesus Christ is truly present in the Eucharist, but too many of them forget this: we are not simply at Mass to receive the Eucharist; we are there to offer the Eucharist too.

Take It to **Prayer**

Father in heaven, we praise you, and we glorify you. We thank you so much. We thank you for the gift of your Son. We thank you for the gift of life. Lord God, often we can overlook the fact that you have given us life. You've called us out of nothing, and you have made us your children. And so often we can overlook the fact that you gave us new life today. You originally gave us a life that we didn't deserve, and you sustain this life that we don't deserve. And we thank you, because this life is good. Even in the valley of tears, this life is good. Because even in the midst of this valley of tears, you come and meet us with your grace. You come and meet us with your Word. You share with us your very life. And even when we carry heavy burdens, Lord God, you have not abandoned us, and you will not abandon us. You are here. And so we ask you, please, come, Lord Jesus. Come and be with your people. Come, Holy Spirit. Come, Father, so that you may be all in all. In Jesus' name we pray. Amen.

Dive **Deeper**

How do the sacraments serve as a glimpse of the heavenly reality that awaits us? Next time you receive Holy Communion, meditate upon eternal life and the beauty of heaven.

Reflect on the **Faith**

- The whole Body of Christ—Jesus Christ the head, the saints in heaven, and the community of the body of Christ—celebrates the Liturgy.

- If you have been baptized, you have been anointed a kingdom priest.

- From our Baptism, we were given a role as kingdom priest—to offer up the sacrifice of the Son to the Father in the power of the Holy Spirit and to praise the Lord.

- The Mass always does two things: glorifies the Father and sanctifies and saves the world.

- When the priest is praying in the name of all the people, we are to unite our hearts and minds to his. If we do this, our participation in the Mass will be transformed, God will be more glorified, the world will be more sanctified, and everything will change.

- We still need the ministerial priesthood, for without the ministerial, ordained priest, we cannot have the sacraments. Jesus gave us those ministerial priests to confect the Eucharist, to give absolution in Reconciliation, and to bring the other sacraments.

- "In liturgical celebrations each person, minister or layman ... should carry out *all* and *only* those parts which pertain to his office by the nature of the rite and the norms of the liturgy" (CCC 1144).

- The pews are not the bleachers. We are not there simply to watch the priest pray. We are there to worship with him. Our job at every Mass is to worship, united with the ministerial priest, and ultimately united with the one great High Priest, Jesus Christ our Lord.

Take It to **Prayer**

Father in heaven, we thank you. We give you praise and glory. You are the God who always remembers. You always remember us. You never forget us, and you could never forget us. Lord God, help us to never forget you. Help us to never forget the work of your hands. Help us to never forget the love that you've shown for us and given to us. Help us always to say yes to you. Help us always to remember as you remember. In Jesus' name we pray. Amen.

Dive **Deeper**

At Mass, take time to imagine the entire Church in heaven worshipping God. How do you picture all the angels, saints, and faithful? Intentionally unite yourself with the entire Mystical Body.

Reflect on the **Faith**

- St. John Paul II said, "The body, and it alone, is capable of making visible what is invisible, the spiritual and divine."[2] We have been given bodies, and through our bodies, we are capable of making visible the invisible.

- Human beings are both soul and body, so we communicate and see "spiritual realities through physical signs and symbols" (CCC 1146).

- We communicate even deep and profound spiritual realities to each other through our bodies—our ears, our hands, our mouths. And "God speaks to man through the visible creation" (CCC 1147). The very reality that creation exists points to a Creator.

- Cleansing, anointing, and sharing food are normal things people would do. But God has given them new meaning, and they become signs of the covenant. Natural things have been given a supernatural power.

- Jesus does physical things to communicate some spiritual healing. He even gives us himself at the Last Supper, and he gives himself up to the Father in the Crucifixion on Golgotha.

- These signs and symbols that Jesus actually did and said have spiritual power. That power is communicated to us in the sacraments.

- When the words and gestures are communicated, these actions that are natural become supernatural. These actions from Jesus that come to us in the sacraments become salvific.

Take It to **Prayer**

Father in heaven, we give you praise. We ask you in the name of your Son, Jesus Christ, to receive our thanksgiving, to receive our praise for you for who you are, for all that you have done. We ask you to please, in the name of your Son, Jesus, send your Holy Spirit out upon us that we can see you, that we can hear your voice. Lord God, in so many ways you have spoken to us. In the most complete and full way, you've spoken to us through your Son. We ask that you please help us to be attuned to his voice. Help us to be attuned to his presence, his action, his reality in this world. Lord, for all the people that we come into contact with today, those we will see, those we have seen, those that are around us in this very moment, we ask you to please bless them as well. Because they are signs of your goodness as well. They are signs of your presence. They are signs of your reality. They were made in your image. And so, help us to just see. Help us to see. To see you and your creation. To see you and the people around us. And to see you in all things. We make this prayer in the mighty name of Jesus Christ, our Lord. Amen.

Dive **Deeper**

THE ALTAR

God communicates spiritual realities to us through sensible signs (see CCC 1146). And thus the liturgy employs many such signs, such as the candles seen adorning the altar in this picture.

Reflect on the **Faith**

- Whenever we celebrate the Eucharist, we encounter the Trinity. This happens in all the sacraments.

- In the fullness of every liturgy, there is always a proclamation of God's Word. The Father, Son, and Holy Spirit speaks to us with words that encourage faith.

- In the Liturgy, there are signs that highlight the role of the Word of God, such as showing reverence with a procession and incense at the proclamation of the Gospel.

- Typically, anyone listening to the Word of God will turn so that the whole body is facing whoever is proclaiming it. This gesture highlights the beauty, power, goodness, and gift that is the Word of God proclaimed in the Liturgy.

- If you have ever felt like you cannot understand Scripture, ask the Holy Spirit to teach you. The Holy Spirit stirs up our faith. He helps us comprehend God's Word. He brings God's amazing deeds to us in the sacraments. What Jesus made possible, the Holy Spirit makes actual.

- We have statues and beautiful buildings and paintings, but out of all the art, music is of highest worth.

- The Church has asked us to use music in the liturgy in order to lift our souls to the Lord and bring us into contact with him.

- Sacred music will lift our souls to the Lord best if it follows three guidelines: it is meant to be prayer, not merely background music; we are all meant to sing at certain points; and it is meant to match the tone of the celebration.

- The whole goal of liturgical music is to give honor to God and make the people of God holy.

Take It to **Prayer**

Father in heaven, we give you praise and glory. We thank you so much for bringing us to this place. We thank you for communicating yourself to us in Sacred Scripture. Thank you for communicating yourself to us through the liturgy, and not just speaking a word from afar, but coming close to us. Thank you for revealing your face and your heart to us in the sacraments. Thank you for speaking to us as to children, inviting us to respond, eliciting some act of faith and of hope and of love back to you who are our good and heavenly Father. Thank you. Please just receive our thanks today that we make in the name of Jesus Christ, our Lord. Amen.

Dive **Deeper**

SACRED MUSIC

The Church values sacred music highly (see CCC 1156).
This photograph shows a book of musical notation for chant.

Reflect on the **Faith**

- Christians use images to help them pray. This is an ancient tradition that is only made possible because of the Incarnation of Jesus Christ.

- Since the Word became flesh and dwelt among us, we can have images of our Savior, the saints, Our Lady, and the angels.

- The iconoclasts wanted to destroy all images of Our Lord, Mary, or the saints—any kind of images that would represent the Lord or holy things—because they saw that as a violation of one of the Ten Commandments.

- The Second Council of Nicaea makes it clear that the Church keeps safe what has been handed down. Among what has been handed down is the practice of making art that shows Jesus. Whether he is shown healing the blind man, on the Cross, or rising from the dead, this art witnesses to historical reality, emphasizing that the Incarnation is not a myth.

- Scripture uses words that are symbols that represent a deeper reality. Artwork is similar. The role of art is meant to unveil, to point to something greater than itself.

- There are "transcendentals": the true, the good, the beautiful. Words and art are meant to reveal the truth, draw us closer to the good, and unveil beauty—to lift the mind and the heart to the Lord. Art does this in a way that words sometimes cannot do.

- We can reason to God's existence, but there are also other ways we communicate the true and the good and the beautiful. This is one of the reasons we decorate our churches with beautiful imagery.

Take It to **Prayer**

Father in heaven, we know that you hear our prayers. We know that you have sent your Son into this world. You've revealed your glory. You have revealed your heart as you've revealed to us your Son. We ask you to, please, continue to reveal your heart to us, continue to unpack the love that you've placed in our hearts by the power of your Holy Spirit. Lord God, help us to see you in all things. In all things that you have created, help us to see your artistic hand. And in all things that artists have created, in every beautiful thing, Lord, let us see a trace, a shadow, a sign of your goodness, of your reality, and of your beauty. Help us to see you in all things today. We make this prayer in the mighty name of Jesus Christ, our Lord. Amen.

Dive **Deeper**

If God is a pure spirit, why is the Father usually depicted in art as an old man with a white beard?

Obviously, God the Father is not literally an old man with a beard. Artwork may show the Father in this way to symbolize various truths about him. In considering this art, we need to remember several things. First, God is *eternal*. He exists outside of time and space and created all things (see CCC 290). Second, God is *personal*. He is not *Something* but *Someone* (see CCC 203). Third, "Jesus revealed that God is Father in an unheard-of sense" (CCC 240). God the Father is the first Person of the Blessed Trinity (see CCC 198).

The apostle Philip asked Jesus to "show us the Father." Jesus replied, "He who has seen me has seen the Father" (John 14:8–9). The Church teaches that in everything that he did and said, Jesus revealed the love and mercy of the Father (see CCC 516, 1701). To know Jesus is to know the Father.

Key reading: CCC 198, 203–204, 238–242, 290–292, 516, 1701

Reflect on the **Faith**

- The big word of the day is *today*. We pray to simply say yes today.

- Liturgical seasons go all the way back to the time of Moses, to the beginnings of the Bible.

- Every Sunday of the year, we celebrate the Lord's resurrection. Each year we have the seasons of Lent, Easter, ordinary time, Advent, and Christmas.

- In the liturgical seasons, the Church pauses to offer thanksgiving to God, ensuring the events of salvation are not forgotten so that people through the ages may learn to act according to God's plan.

- We cannot go back and change the past or go into the future. All we are given to work with is now. The liturgical season reminds us of this fact. It reminds us that there is something that is on its way, but we are called to live today.

- This helps us even when we look at our sins. We can look back and wish things were different and be trapped there. The Church asks us to surrender that past to the Lord and live right now, today.

- We celebrate on Sunday because of the Resurrection; it is the day the Lord rose from the dead. We have the ability to live "without fear" today because of what Jesus Christ did for us on Sunday (CCC 1167).

Take It to **Prayer**

Father in heaven, you have given us this day. You've given us this day to say yes to you. You've given us this day to say yes to your mercy. You've given us this day to say yes to your courage. You've given us this day to say yes to hope. And we ask you to, please—in this moment and wherever we are at right now—we ask you, please, open up our hearts, open up our minds so that we don't delay anymore, so we don't say "later," we don't say "tomorrow," but we simply say yes, today. Now, Lord, now is the time. This day is the day. Help us to give you our whole yes, our whole heart, our whole selves right now, in this moment, today. We make this prayer in Jesus' name. Amen.

Dive **Deeper**

We can only encounter God in the present moment. Focus today on the things happening right now and surrender the future to Jesus. Pray the Litany of Trust, which can be found online from the Sisters of Life. If you would like to watch a video and pray along with the sisters, you can find it on the Ascension Presents YouTube video "Pray with Us: The Litany of Trust (feat. The Sisters of Life)."

Reflect on the **Faith**

- The liturgical year highlights the big feasts that we celebrate every single year. It is very cyclical.

- The Easter Triduum is number one: Holy Thursday, Good Friday, Holy Saturday, and Easter Sunday. Those days are the holiest days of the Church year because Jesus' suffering, death, and resurrection are what saves us.

- The Eucharist is not only Christ's action; it is Christ himself. What Jesus did on the Cross is the heart of everything.

- The method of finding the date of Easter was determined during the Council of Nicaea in AD 325.

- Since those in the East and West figure out the date in different ways, we do not celebrate Easter on the exact same day as Orthodox Christians.

- Other major feasts over the course of the year celebrate the Incarnation, such as the Annunciation, Christmas, and Epiphany.

- We also have in the liturgical year the "sanctoral" as we commemorate the Blessed Virgin Mary—whose yes to the Lord is unparalleled—and the saints and martyrs, who remind us that we have a family.

- We are called to ask, how has the Lord worked in those people's lives? He has taken ordinary people and made them extraordinary. He has taken broken people like you and me and made them saints.

- God has made you and me to be saints. He has redeemed you and me to be nothing less than a saint of God who gives him glory for all eternity.

- We can start this right now by giving him glory *today*.

Take It to **Prayer**

Father in heaven, we give you praise. We give you glory. You are the God of heaven and earth. You are the God who made all time. You are the God who made all space. You are the God of it all. And we ask you to please not only sanctify all that you've created, not only sanctify all the space you've created, all the places you've created—sanctify time. Sanctify our time this day, Lord God. Let this day be a day that is consecrated to you, a day that is dedicated and set apart for you. No matter when we're listening to this, Lord God, let this day be your day. And may you be glorified in the ordinary. May you be glorified in the normal. May you be glorified this day and every day. In Jesus' name we pray. Amen.

Dive **Deeper**

RAVENNA LITURGICAL CALENDAR

In the feasts of the liturgy, the Church proposes to the faithful a way of entering into the Paschal Mystery throughout the year (see CCC 1171). This photograph shows a marble liturgical calendar for the years AD 532–626 found in Ravenna, Italy.

Reflect on the **Faith**

- The Liturgy of the Hours is also known as the Divine Office. It is the prayer of the Church, for priests, religious, and all the faithful.

- It is prayed five times a day, to sanctify the day: the Office of Readings, Morning Prayer, Daytime Prayer, Evening Prayer, and Night Prayer.

- The Liturgy of the Hours exists to assist all of us to do exactly what the Scriptures have commanded us: to pray always.

- We set aside time at various points in each day to encounter God's Word and let the Lord speak to us, and then we speak back to him.

- God made time and, because of that, time can be holy. As Christians, we are called to consecrate time. No matter who we are or how big our home is, we can all set aside time that is holy to the Lord.

- The Liturgy of the Hours is meant to help us participate (as part of the kingdom priesthood) in the offering of the Eucharist during the week, even if we are unable to get to Mass on other days besides Sunday.

- The Liturgy of the Hours is the prayer of the whole Church.

- This is not meant to diminish the importance of other prayers—such as the Rosary, the Chaplet of Divine Mercy, or the Stations of the Cross.

- Start choosing one of the prayers to do each day. To make it easier, there are apps to download and podcasts of people recorded praying the Liturgy of the Hours.

- Remember that each hour of the day, you are a kingdom priest. Pray the Liturgy of the Hours to see what it feels like to sanctify each hour of the day.

Take It to **Prayer**

Father in heaven, we give you thanks and praise. We ask you to please send your Holy Spirit to be with us now. Send your Holy Spirit to fill our minds and our hearts. Lord, especially in Jesus' name, I ask you to cast out any spirit of false guilt that anyone who's joining us today might be experiencing, that false guilt where I feel like I'm doing something wrong—I'm not doing anything wrong. Where I feel like I'm not doing enough when, no, I'm doing exactly what you're asking me to do. Lord God, in the name of Jesus, your Son, cast out that spirit of false guilt. Give us a true sense of guilt. Give us a true awareness of where it is you're calling us to act, where you're calling us to speak, where you're calling us to refrain from acting or speaking. But, Lord, help us in our weakness, help us in our ignorance, help us in our blindness and our deafness to be able to silence that voice of false guilt and to be attentive to the Holy Spirit who convicts us and leads us into all truth. In Jesus' name we pray. Amen.

Dive **Deeper**

Before bed tonight, pray Night Prayer from the Liturgy of the Hours. By doing this you are uniting yourself with the Church's prayer.

Reflect on the **Faith**

- We are spatial beings, and the Lord is worshipped in space as well as in time. He is worshipped everywhere, notably in churches.

- Wherever the People of God are gathered, that is where the Church is. Wherever the bishop is, that is where the Church is.

- In the two thousand years of the Church, many Catholics have been persecuted—and even today there are many places where Catholics are not allowed to gather in a church. Wherever we gather for the Eucharist, that place is holy. And where Christians are free to do so, churches are built.

- There needs to be an altar in the church, for Jesus offered himself on the altar of the Cross. It "is also the table of the Lord, to which the People of God are invited" (CCC 1182).

- There needs to be a Tabernacle, where the Eucharist is reserved, in a visible, prominent place of honor and adoration.

- Holy oils—sacred chrism and the oil of catechumens—are present, for use in anointing at Baptism and Confirmation and for the sick.

- The bishop's or priest's chair indicates his role in the gathering, and the lectern or ambo is where the Word of God is proclaimed and explained.

- There must be suitable places for Baptism and Confession, as well as space for prayer and reflection.

- Places for socializing are welcome in the church but should be separated from spaces for prayer.

Take It to **Prayer**

Father in heaven, we do give you praise. In the name of your Son, Jesus Christ, we ask you to receive our praise and thanksgiving. Your Son, Jesus, who is God, fully God, and yet, at one moment, he entered into time. At one moment, he entered into space in a unique way in the Incarnation. Lord God, in the same way, we ask that you please, once again, break into our time. Break into our space. Break into our lives with your goodness, with your grace, with your Holy Spirit. Renew us and sanctify each moment of our days. And sanctify each place that our feet tread. Lord God, we ask you to send your Holy Spirit upon our local church, our local parish. We ask you to fill that space with your Holy Spirit. And may it become more and more a place where you are worshipped and the People of God are sanctified. We make this prayer in the mighty name of Jesus Christ, our Lord. Amen.

Dive **Deeper**

CHRIST AND THE WOMAN OF SAMARIA AT THE WELL
BY GIOVANNI FRANCESCO BARBIERI

This painting depicts Jesus' meeting with the Samaritan woman at the well, during which he tells her that God is to be worshipped "in spirit and truth" (John 4:24; see CCC 1179).

Reflect on the **Faith**

- Christ is the one who celebrates the liturgy, as our High Priest who is constantly offering himself to the Father.

- The Father and Son pour themselves out to each other in love, and that love between them is the person of the Holy Spirit.

- All the angels and saints in heaven are drawn into the worship of the Holy Trinity, into that sacrifice and offering of love.

- The altar is where time and eternity meet, and we get to participate in it.

- The sacraments are not empty rituals nor mere expressions of prayers read out of a book, but rather they are a real participation on earth of what is happening in eternity.

- As we listen to the words of the liturgy, the angels and saints are in heaven glorifying the Father continually.

- The Liturgy of the Hours is called the prayer of the Church because it is an extension of Christ's priesthood onto this earth in which all who share in the baptismal priesthood can participate.

- The Mass is the most perfect form in which we can participate in the work of Christ, but praying the Liturgy of the Hours is also a participation in the prayers and the priesthood of Jesus Christ.

Take It to **Prayer**

Father in heaven, we praise you. We give you glory. We thank you for bringing us to this day. We ask that you please send your Holy Spirit to not only remind us of what you have done; remind us of what you've taught us and told us, revealed to us through your Word, in Scripture and through your holy Church; remind us of all of these things; but also fill us with insight. Give us wisdom, not just knowledge. Give us even more. Give us the practical knowledge, practical wisdom to be able to worship you well and walk with you in faith and hope and in love. We make this prayer in the mighty name of Jesus Christ, our Lord. Amen.

Dive **Deeper**

Reflect upon the significance of genuflection. How does this sign signify the kingship of Christ? Do we genuflect out of habit or out of reverence for God?

Reflect on the **Faith**

- There are a number of rites in the Roman Catholic Church, allowing both a diversity and unity in the same Church.

- Different rites celebrate the sacraments in unique forms, but this is never a uniqueness that is completely foreign to us.

- The rich history in other more ancient rites, such as the Byzantine, Alexandrian, or Coptic, is significantly beautiful, and yet it takes nothing away from the Church's overall unity.

- The Church's different rites came about because of her mission to go into all nations and make disciples, baptizing them in the name of the Father, Son, and Holy Spirit.

- The Apostles and their successors were sent out to bring the sacraments and, as missionaries, encountered various cultures. This led to a variety of ways in which the sacraments, from the same source, could grow.

- The various liturgies are like the same kind of fruit grown in different types of soil, so looking slightly different in the end.

- In other times and places, the Eucharist may historically have been reserved in a vessel shaped like a dove, unlike our square tabernacles today.

- There are traditions and rites in the Church that have emphasized some ways of becoming holy that are not as emphasized in other rites. But it is all the same mission.

Take It to **Prayer**

God in heaven, we love you, and we thank you. We thank you for the way in which you have brought about a unity and a diversity, a variety and a catholicity, universality. Lord God, you have given us this cosmic world, this world that is so diverse and yet is one world. You've given us this Church that is so diverse, and yet it's one Church. And you've made us, Lord God, individuals who are so unique. And yet we are one, united into one Body in Christ. Lord God, you're the God of variety and unity. You're the God of uniqueness and oneness. And so we come before you as we are, as individuals. But we also come before you as a Body. We come before you as individual persons, but we also come before you as your Church. And we just lift up our minds and our hearts to you right now and ask you to send your Holy Spirit to fill our individual hearts and minds. But also to unite us even more closely as one Body, in the name of your Son, Jesus Christ, our Lord. Amen.

Dive **Deeper**

Can a Roman Catholic receive communion at an Eastern rite Mass?

Yes. The Code of Canon Law clearly states that a Roman Catholic can receive communion at any Eastern Catholic Rite Mass (see CIC 923).

There are over one billion Catholics in the world, many of whom belong to one of the twenty-three Eastern Catholic churches. These include the Ruthenian Church, the Armenian Catholic Church, and the Coptic Catholic Church. Many follow the Byzantine rite, while others follow other rites. All of these Eastern Catholic Churches are in full communion with the pope and have valid sacraments. As St. Paul VI declared, "Between these [churches] there exists an admirable bond of union, such that the variety within the Church in no way harms its unity; rather it manifests it, for it is the mind of the Catholic Church that each individual Church or Rite should retain its traditions whole and entire and likewise that it should adapt its way of life to the different needs of time and place" (*Orientalium Ecclesiarum* 2).

Key Readings: St. Paul VI, Decree on the Catholic Churches of the Eastern Rite: *Orientalium Ecclesiarum*

Reflect on the **Faith**

- The Church incorporates the culture in a unique way when celebrating the liturgy, while ensuring there is no corruption to the liturgy.

- Liturgical rites grew up because of the Church's mission: to engage every people and go to all nations. There is no culture, individual, race, ethnicity, or language that does not deserve to know the Good News of Jesus Christ.

- With this mission, the Church has gone to all the world proclaiming the Good News. It brings the seed, the gifts of the sacraments and liturgy. Heaven and earth, time and eternity touch.

- Some cultural images that were originally pagan (such as Christmas trees) can be "adopted" in a way as signs of Christianity. Like us, they are brought into the Lord, into the Body of Christ.

- Yet some things are not compatible with the Church and our Faith, and they cannot be integrated. We must be faithful to apostolic Tradition.

- While some parts of the liturgy in the different rites can be changed, there is an unchangeable aspect of those rites that is put in place by God.

- The Church must protect what cannot be changed—and sometimes the Church is called to change what is changeable.

- Part of the continued missionary command from Jesus Christ given to all of us today is to proclaim the Gospel.

- We also must pray as best we can in the way that was given to us by the Church, to be faithful to Tradition and give God glory and prayer for the sanctification and salvation of the world.

Take It to **Prayer**

Father in heaven, we give you praise and glory. Thank you so much for bringing us to this day. We ask you to please enlighten our minds; open our hearts so that we can appreciate the variety that you've given to us and that we can participate in the unity of the Church that you have given to us through your beloved Son, our Lord Jesus Christ. In the name of the Father, and of the Son, and of the Holy Spirit. Amen.

Dive **Deeper**

Did you know the Catholic Church has many rites of the liturgy? Spend time learning about the different rites in the Church. If available, search for a local Eastern rite Catholic Liturgy to attend.

Reflect on the **Faith**

- There are seven sacraments: sacraments of initiation (Baptism, Confirmation, Holy Eucharist), healing (Reconciliation and the Anointing of the Sick), and mission or service (Holy Orders and Holy Matrimony).

- "The sacraments of Christian initiation ... lay the *foundations* of every Christian life" (CCC 1212).

- Baptism brings us into relationship with God and makes us into God's very children.

- In the Eucharist, we are strengthened and given the very life of Jesus Christ, his own Body, Blood, Soul, and Divinity.

- In Confirmation, we experience the further outpouring of the Holy Spirit that Jesus poured out on the Apostles at Pentecost.

- Originally, many were baptized by being fully submerged. Today, we also often use the pouring of water to effect the sacrament of Baptism.

- Baptism causes a new birth.

- All of the sacraments are accompanied by the Word of God proclaimed, which enlightens every person. The person baptized is now a child of the light.

- God reveals himself in nature. He slowly continued to reveal himself in the Old Covenant to Abraham, Moses, and the people of God. From the beginning, he has used water in powerful ways.

- Springs of water can represent life, while deep waters can represent death. The symbolism comes together in Jesus. We have been baptized into Christ's death, and in that Baptism, we are given his life.

- God uses water in the saving of his people, such as when he saves Noah and his family during the Flood or when he saves the Israelites from the Egyptians at the Red Sea.

Take It to **Prayer**

Father in heaven, you are good, and you are God. And you have made us your children through the waters of Baptism. You made us your children by the action of your Son in the pouring out of your Holy Spirit upon this world. Lord God, come once again into our hearts. Come once again in your Holy Spirit to give us your divine life so that we can be truly your sons and daughters; we truly can be regenerated; we truly can be born again in you. Lord Jesus, your mercies are new every morning. Come and meet us with your mercy now. Father in heaven, you send out your Holy Spirit through the name of your Son, Jesus. Send out your Holy Spirit now, once again, and renew the face of the earth. We make this prayer in the mighty name of Jesus Christ, our Lord. Amen.

Dive **Deeper**

Baptism is an essential part of initiation into the Church. Without Baptism, we are unable to receive the other sacraments. Watch the Ascension Presents YouTube video "Why Baptizing Your Baby Is the Most Important Thing You Can Do" to dive deeper into the significance of Baptism in the Church.

Reflect on the **Faith**

- Jesus has given us, through the power of the Holy Spirit, Baptism in the Church. On Pentecost, St. Peter proclaimed that all should repent and be baptized.

- Jesus is the fulfillment of every one of God's promises from the Old Testament.

- The baptism of St. John the Baptist was a baptism of repentance for sinful people. Yet Jesus himself, who had no need to repent, allowed himself to be baptized. He "fulfill[s] all righteousness" in his "self-emptying" (CCC 1224).

- Pope Benedict reflected on the crowd of people who had come out to see Jesus be baptized by John. Jesus gets baptized not because he needs it but because *they* need it. He brings them into the waters with him.

- The waters do not make Jesus holy; he makes the waters holy. And now the waters of Baptism make *us* holy.

- Jesus takes the incredible image and symbolism of the baptism that John was doing and gives it new meaning and power. Baptism was a reality that existed, and Jesus took it and transformed it. From now on, Baptism saves us.

- Baptism makes us into temples of the Holy Spirit. In the Church from the very beginning, Christians understood that Baptism is what saves us. Now, Jesus Christ himself has transformed and given a new power to the Old Covenant baptism.

- In chapter 3 of the Gospel of John, Jesus says we must be born of water and the Spirit to enter God's Kingdom. Baptism is not just important but necessary.

- At one point, we need to embrace our own faith and Baptism. We all now can renew that commitment and those baptismal promises through the power of the Holy Spirit.

Take It to **Prayer**

Father in heaven, we praise you, and we ask that you—we thank you, Father, we thank you for the gift of Baptism. We thank you for the gift of your Holy Spirit that has washed away our sins. We thank you for the gift of your Holy Spirit that has made us into your children, into your sons and into your daughters. Thank you for the gift of your Holy Spirit that enables us to cry out "Abba, Father." Only by the Spirit can we cry out "Abba, Father." Only by the Spirit can we be your children. We thank you. Jesus, we thank you for being baptized and extending that Baptism, retransforming that baptism and making it into something entirely new. And we thank you, Holy Spirit, for coming to us, for sanctifying the waters of Baptism, coming close to every one of us—so close that you have made us into temples of this Holy Spirit. So God, we just praise you. Father, Son, and Holy Spirit, may you be glorified and loved, adored and worshipped for all time and into eternity. In Jesus' name we pray. In the name of the Father, and of the Son, and of the Holy Spirit. Amen.

Dive **Deeper**

JESUS BEING BAPTIZED

*Here we see Jesus baptized in the Jordan by John the Baptist.
This event signals the beginning of Jesus' public ministry (see CCC 1223).*

Reflect on the **Faith**

- On Pentecost, Peter told people that to be saved they must repent and be baptized. Thousands of people were baptized that day. As the Church continued to spread, it became clear that there needed to be a more thorough process.

- The Jewish people had been shaped by the Old Testament, so their step into accepting Jesus as the Messiah made sense.

- As the Church continues to expand, there are people who do not know there is one God or that we are made in God's image and likeness. This requires a dramatic conversion to see the world through the lens of Jesus.

- Often in the West, especially in the Catholic Church, Baptism happens right away. We are brought into the Church before the age of reason. Because of that, there must be a "*post-baptismal catechumenate*" (CCC 1231).

- In the Eastern rites, infants are baptized, confirmed, and given the Holy Eucharist at once. In the Roman or Latin rite, usually we are baptized as infants then later go on to First Reconciliation and Holy Communion and then to Confirmation.

- If we walk in faith, live in hope, and choose to love, those are great signs of the Holy Spirit in our lives.

Take It to **Prayer**

*Father in heaven, we thank you, and we give you praise. In the name
of your Son, Jesus Christ, receive our praise, receive our thanks this day.
Lord God, in the midst of sorrow, in the midst of joy, in the midst of suffering,
and in the midst of strength, we just give you praise. And we ask that you please
hear our prayer and throw out your Holy Spirit upon all of us, that those of us
who are on our way into full initiation with the Catholic Church may get to that
place with great joy and great love. And for those who have been initiated into
the Church, into your Church, we ask that you awaken in our hearts and enliven in
our lives your grace. Your grace is new every morning. Your mercies are new every
morning. And you are here with us now. Bring those graces to life. Ignite them.
Like a smoldering wick or a burning ember, let them become a roaring flame.
We make this prayer in the mighty name of Jesus Christ, our Lord. Amen.*

Dive **Deeper**

If someone is not validly baptized, would that mean that any other sacraments
he or she received would be invalid?

Yes. According to the Code of Canon Law, a person who has not been baptized
cannot validly receive the other sacraments (see CIC 842). The sacrament of
Baptism brings with it rights and responsibilities, including the ability to be
part of the sacramental life of the Church, be nourished with the Word of God,
and be sustained by the other spiritual helps of the Church. So if a person is
not validly baptized, any other sacraments he or she might receive would be
invalid—and the person would need to receive them again after being baptized.

Key reading: CCC 1269

Reflect on the **Faith**

- Mystagogy is the unpacking or the teaching of the mystery.

- By tracing the Sign of the Cross on the child's forehead and inviting the parents and godparents to do the same in the Latin rite, we claim the child being baptized for Jesus Christ.

- God's Word is read because our reaction to his Word must be faith, and the sacrament of Baptism is "the sacrament of faith" (CCC 1236).

- Then there is a rite of exorcism. We recognize that we are born under the dominion of the Evil One. We need to be transferred from the kingdom of darkness to the kingdom of God. The exorcism calls upon the name of our Lord Jesus Christ and explicitly renounces Satan.

- Later there is anointing with chrism and use of a white garment and candle.

- Baptism transfers us from the kingdom of darkness to the kingdom of life. It brings about a death of sin and new life in Jesus. Our sins are forgiven. We are adopted as God's beloved sons and daughters.

- The next steps are preparation for our First Holy Communion and Confirmation. In the Eastern Church, when a child is baptized, he or she is immediately chrismated or confirmed and receives Holy Communion. In the West, these sacraments happen later on.

- Baptism is just the first step. A person realizes he or she is not alone and needs to continue to walk as a child of God.

- We acknowledge that Baptism, when we were made an adopted son or daughter, was not the end. And we ask God how he wants us to walk today, in courage, faith, hope, and love, justice, fortitude, prudence and temperance, generosity, graciousness, patience.

Take It to **Prayer**

Father in heaven, we give you thanks. We praise you for your glory. We praise you for who you are. We thank you. We thank you for the gift of Baptism. We thank you for the gift of not only declaring us to be your children but making us into your children. We thank you for allowing us to have access to your father's heart. We thank you for giving us your only beloved Son as our Savior, our Lord, our God, and our brother. We thank you for your Holy Spirit that dwells in us. Thank you for making us the temple of your Holy Spirit. Lord God, as we unpack the mystery of the celebration of Baptism, we ask that you please give us a fire of love, a fire of faith and hope, a fire that wants to rekindle what you placed in our hearts at our own baptism. Give us a love for you that will never end, so that in you our lives will never end. In Jesus' name we pray. Amen.

Dive **Deeper**

Do you know your baptism birthday? Reflect upon the significance of your spiritual birth and take time to renew your baptismal promises today.

Reflect on the **Faith**

- The Church tells us that "every person not yet baptized" can receive this sacrament (CCC 1246). Baptism is for everyone. It is God's free grace.

- God's grace of salvation and redemption is meant to be inclusive. God wants all men to be saved. He wants those who do not know of Jesus Christ to know of him.

- A lot of people are raised without hearing the Good News of Jesus Christ. Because of that, there is the "catechumenate" or preparation. It should be "a formation in the whole Christian life" (CCC 1248). God's Word is preached, and the person accepts it with faith.

- We baptize infants because humans are fallen and have experienced original sin. We are under the dominion of darkness and need God's grace.

- God's goodness is revealed because the infant has done nothing to merit this grace. And yet God pours out his love. If we were to keep a child from the grace of Baptism, we would be withholding an amazing gift.

- The Church says that anyone not already baptized can be baptized, either as adults or infants.

- God's grace of redemption is not exclusive, as he reveals that he wants all men to know him and be saved.

- If you have already been baptized, then God is calling you, as a temple of the Holy Spirit, to spread his Word to the whole world.

- We ought to praise the Lord for the formation in the Christian life that we have already had, and for how it will lead us further to becoming the people God has called us to be.

Take It to **Prayer**

Father in heaven, we praise you. We give you glory, and we thank you. Thank you for the gift of Baptism. If we have received Baptism, we just praise you because this gift has come to us—a purely gratuitous gift, a purely gracious gift, a grace-filled gift, an undeserved gift, an unearned gift, a gift that comes from your heart. We thank you. And for all of us who are listening who have not been baptized, we ask that you please lead us step-by-step closer and closer to this incredible gift that you have in store. You want everyone—you want everyone on this planet, everyone who has ever lived, is living, or will live. You want them to be brought into your family. And so we ask you, please, Lord God, for all those who are listening, joining us today, and walking with us who are not baptized, we ask that you lead them by the power of your love and your truth to the fountain of Baptism so they can also become sons and daughters of you, our heavenly Father. We make this prayer in the mighty name of Jesus Christ, our Lord. Amen.

Dive **Deeper**

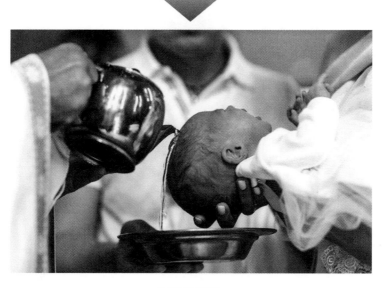

BAPTISM

Infant baptism shows in a powerful way the completely free gift of God's saving grace (see CCC 1250).

Reflect on the **Faith**

- Faith and Baptism are inherently linked.

- In the Gospel of Mark chapter 2, we read about the paralyzed man whose four friends brought him to Jesus. Scripture says, "When Jesus saw their faith, he said to the paralytic, 'Child, your sins are forgiven'" (Mark 2:5). This is a case where the faith of someone else has spoken on behalf of the person who is forgiven. That is what we have when it comes to infant Baptism.

- Bishops, priests, and deacons are all "ordinary ministers of Baptism" in our Latin Church. "In case of necessity, anyone … can baptize" as long as the person intends "to do what the Church does when she baptizes" and uses water and the words of Baptism in the name of the Holy Trinity (CCC 1256).

- In John 3:5, Jesus says, "Unless one is born of water and the Spirit, he cannot enter the kingdom of God," confirming the necessity of Baptism.

- God is in charge of all things and knows everything vastly more than any of us could ever hope to understand. God is the one who gave us the sacrament of Baptism, and God is also the one who said that this is the way to be saved; he has not given us another way.

- The *Catechism* also says, "*God has bound salvation to the sacrament of Baptism, but he himself is not bound by his sacraments*" (CCC 1257).

- Since Christ died to save every person, we can hold onto the belief that God makes it possible in some way for every person to have a chance to say yes to him.

- We have funerals for children who were not baptized in order to pray for them, and we only pray for people when we have hope for them to be in heaven.

- Let us continue to live and walk in God's love.

Take It to **Prayer**

Father in heaven, we come before you, and we give you this day. We give you all the joys and sorrows of this day. We give you all the victories and frustrations of this day. We give you the work and the rest of this day. Let it all be for you. Let it all be a gift to you because this day has been your gift to us. And so, as we come before you, we do not want to come before you empty-handed. Lord God, even our failures we bring to you. Even our sins we bring to you. We all want to bring to you those things we're proud of and those wins, that great work. And you accept those, but you also accept our weaknesses. You also accept our failures. You also accept our sins. We bring it all to you. The good days and the bad days. The victories and the losses. It is all yours because you are the Lord. Truly, you are the Lord of everything, including the Lord of everything in our lives and everything today. So please accept it all and accept it in the name of your Son, Jesus Christ, our Lord. We make this prayer in the mighty name of Jesus, in the name of the Father, and of the Son, and of the Holy Spirit. Amen.

Dive **Deeper**

What happens to children who die before baptism?

God has entrusted the Church with the sacraments as the "ordinary" means of imparting saving grace—but his mercy and grace are not limited to them. So, without diminishing the essential nature of Baptism as the gateway to salvation, the Church entrusts these children "to the mercy of God, as she does in her funeral rites for them. Indeed, the great mercy of God ... and Jesus' tenderness toward children ... allow us to hope that there is a way of salvation for children who have died without Baptism" (CCC 1261). While "there is not an explicit teaching on this question found in Revelation," we can find "there are theological and liturgical reasons to hope that infants who die without baptism may be saved and brought into eternal happiness ... [and] there are reasons to hope that God will save these infants precisely because it was not possible ... to baptize them.[3] The Church does not give a definitive answer to the question of children who are lost before Baptism, therefore.

Key reading: CCC 1261

Reflect on the **Faith**

- In Baptism, the submersion into water represents both dying and washing. We cannot change the symbol of the sacrament without changing its meaning, and that is why water is essential to Baptism.

- Many people in the early Church were tempted to put off Baptism until the end of their lives in order to be newly purified when they died, but we don't know when we are going to die, and the Lord wants to bring us into eternal life now rather than later.

- Every person who lives on this earth is a beloved creature of God. But something has to change in us and our human nature in order for us to actually be sons and daughters of God.

- We have to "become partakers of the divine nature" (2 Peter 1:4). When we receive the Holy Spirit in Baptism, God changes our nature. We become a new kind of a being.

- In the Old Covenant, the people would call God "Father" by analogy. Now, in the New Covenant, we can call God "Father" because he has adopted us.

- It cost God the death of his eternal, only begotten Son to adopt us and pour out his Holy Spirit for this great gift. Baptism is not just a ritual or sign. It transforms, heals, forgives, and makes us new.

- Even though we are forgiven of original sin and our personal sins, we still suffer the "temporal consequences of sin," including pain, sickness, death, and attraction to sin, called "concupiscence" (CCC 1264). But we can resist sin with God's help.

Take It to **Prayer**

Father in heaven, you send out your Holy Spirit among us. And you've given us your Holy Spirit through the great sacrament of Baptism. This is the beginnings, the doorway, to faith. We ask that you, please, as you poured your Holy Spirit into our lives through the sacrament of Baptism, continue to pour your Holy Spirit throughout the rest of our lives, into eternity, throughout this whole world. Lord God, we pray that every person on this planet will come to know you; that every person on this planet will come to know of your incredible love, unstoppable love, your faithful love for them. And we ask that you please help us to understand this. Help us to understand your love in a deeper and deeper way this day and every day. In Jesus' name we pray. Amen.

Dive **Deeper**

JESUS WITH THE PHARISEE NICODEMUS

Jesus spoke to Nicodemus about the mystery of Baptism, by which we are spiritually reborn and made new creations in Christ (see CCC 1265; John 3:1–30).

Reflect on the **Faith**

- Through Baptism, we are each brought into the Body of Christ, entering the New Covenant with God.

- In the Old Covenant, the Jewish people were brought into an intimate relationship with God as a holy people. In the New Covenant, every part of the Old Covenant is fulfilled.

- A baptized person has both real obligations and real rights as a Catholic.

- Priests are obliged to hear anyone's confession if the person asks within reason, because one of the rights of being a Catholic is to be fed by Scripture and the sacraments.

- We have an obligation to speak out about the Faith and spread the Good News.

- When we look at the world and see a loss of belief and morals, we can ask what the leaders have done wrong, but the only level we can directly influence is our own level. So we have to look at our lives and ask if we have abdicated from our calling to speak out about the Faith.

- Every person who has been validly baptized is a son or daughter of God. We are truly brothers and sisters, even if we have an imperfect relationship with each other.

- Through Baptism, we have an "indelible spiritual mark" that means we are Christ's forever (CCC 1272).

- We can freely choose not to live in the Father's house, but no sin can undo the mark of our Baptism and make the Father abandon us. This mark is a gift, but we are still called to use it.

Take It to **Prayer**

Father in heaven, we give you praise and glory. We thank you so much for the gift of your Son, Jesus Christ, the gift of your Holy Spirit you've poured out on the face of this earth, and you've poured it into our hearts. We ask you to please unite us even more perfectly to your Church. Unite us even more perfectly to each other. Help us to see that we belong to each other, not only by virtue of our belonging to the human race but even more particularly and even more powerfully, that we belong to each other because of our fellowship, our friendship, and even our brotherhood in the fact that you have made us into your sons and daughters. Help us to know that you are our Father. Help us to live as if we are truly brothers and sisters. We make this prayer in the mighty name of Jesus Christ, our Lord. Amen.

Dive **Deeper**

Through Baptism, we become part of the People of God, and therefore we will always belong. Do you feel like you belong or "fit in" at church? Reflect on how you can grow in community with those at your local parish.

Reflect on the **Faith**

- None of us has done anything to earn having our sins forgiven. In fact, Jesus has done it all, and our approaching the sacraments is our response.

- Reconciliation and Holy Communion, which we more frequently repeat, highlight the fact that God is actively seeking us and inviting us to participate in his new life. Our participation is our yes to the Lord.

- When we come to confession, it is not us begging God to give us another chance. It is God begging us to give his mercy another chance.

- Every one of the effects of Baptism is worth pondering and praying with.

- We praise God for bringing us into his own kingdom, forgiving all our sins, and making us his children.

- Through Baptism, we also participate in Christ's role as priest, so there is not one aspect of our lives that we cannot offer up to the Father.

- Jesus' death and resurrection in the Paschal Mystery is the culmination, but every moment of Jesus' life was an offering in obedience to the Father.

- As we share in the holy priesthood, in the Mass, we get to participate in the great sacrifice of the Son to the Father in the Eucharist and the power of the Holy Spirit in a unique way.

Take It to **Prayer**

Father in heaven, we give you praise and glory. Thank you for joy. Thank you for laughter. Thank you for—in the midst of the day of our lives, the days of our lives, the sufferings of each day and the ordinariness of each day—we thank you for giving us the joy of new life. Thank you for giving us the joy of your Son. Thank you for giving us the joy of the Holy Spirit and knowing, Lord God, even in the midst of our worst days, our worst seasons, that we have you, and you're present to us. Help us to be aware of your presence. Help us to respond to your presence and your invitation by saying yes to you in all things. Help us say yes to you in the wins and in the victories. Help us say yes to you in the losses, in the failures. In the midst of our sin, Lord God, help us to say yes to you so that by your grace we may be lifted up and brought back to your heart. In Jesus' name we pray. Amen.

Dive **Deeper**

God has adopted you as his beloved child. Do you feel like you belong to him? Spend time giving God thanks for freely adopting you into his family.

Reflect on the **Faith**

- Everyone who has been baptized has received God's grace and the Holy Spirit, but "the reception of the sacrament of Confirmation is necessary for the completion of baptismal grace" (CCC 1285).

- Confirmation unites a baptized person more completely to the Church. The Apostles themselves needed the gift of the Holy Spirit at Pentecost.

- Before Jesus ascended to heaven, he promised to give the Holy Spirit to the Apostles and disciples. He said, "You shall receive power when the Holy Spirit has come upon you; and you shall be my witnesses in Jerusalem and in all Judea and Samaria and to the end of the earth" (Acts 1:8). The Greek word for "witnesses" is *martyres*, which is where we get the word "martyr."

- This power from the Holy Spirit is a power "to spread and defend the faith by word and action ... to confess the name of Christ boldly, and never to be ashamed of the Cross" (CCC 1303).

- Jesus himself is active in his Apostles. In his humility, he not only became human and was crucified, but he called his disciples to be filled with the Holy Spirit to carry out the mission he began. If they do not share the Gospel, the mission fails.

- In the sacrament of Confirmation, we too are filled with the power of the Spirit to better share Christ's mission with the world, and this mission will also stop without us as witnesses. Confirmation mirrors Pentecost.

- Jesus Christ is the Anointed One, and the coming of the Holy Spirit was an anointing. The Church came to use the holy oil of chrism, blessed by the bishop, in the sacrament of Confirmation, as a fitting symbol.

Take It to **Prayer**

Father in heaven, we thank you. We give you praise, and we just cry out in the power of your Holy Spirit, that great are you, Lord. Great are you, Father. You are so good, and you continue to give us your grace every single day. Thank you for helping us press play today. Honestly, thank you, Lord, for bringing us to day 175, where we can hear more and more about the love you have for your people, the love you have for your children, and the way in which you want to pour out your Spirit. Make us all prophets. Give us all a share in your priesthood. Give us a share in your Spirit of prophecy. Give us a share in your royal gift, your royal office. You've called us to be members of your family. You've made us your sons and daughters. Help us to live like this this day and every day. In Jesus' name we pray. Amen.

Dive **Deeper**

PENTECOST

This artwork depicts Pentecost, when the Holy Spirit came to empower the followers of Christ to go out boldly into the world and preach the Gospel. We, too, receive the power and grace of the Holy Spirit in the sacrament of Confirmation (see CCC 1288).

Reflect on the **Faith**

- Both the Eastern and Western rites of Confirmation include the anointing with sacred chrism blessed by the bishop, and the imprinting of the seal of the Holy Spirit on the person claimed by Jesus Christ.

- Before a person is baptized, he or she is anointed with oil. This part of the rite talks about a transfer from being under the dominion of the Evil One to that of the Lord. Making clean and making strong are represented by the anointing.

- There are two sacraments in which a person is anointed after Baptism: Confirmation and Holy Orders. When a person is anointed in either of these sacraments, that person is made holy and set apart.

- At the end of John's Gospel, we read that Jesus sends the Apostles forth on mission, breathing on them and bestowing upon them the Holy Spirit and the ability to forgive sins. (See John 20:21–23.)

- Jesus' mission was to bring hope to a world in darkness and grace to a world that did not know grace. He brought the mercy of God to a people that needed it and the truth to those who were ignorant of it.

- Being sealed by the Holy Spirit shows that we are entirely Christ's.

- The thought that your heart is marked to show you are fully under ownership might be initially unpleasant, but the reality is that all of us are called to walk in the Lord and be claimed.

- If we have been baptized and confirmed, none of us belong to ourselves anymore. We belong to God completely.

Take It to **Prayer**

Father in heaven, we give you glory, and we praise your name. We thank you for the outpouring of your Holy Spirit. We thank you for the gift and the grace of Confirmation. We thank you for making us your sons and daughters in Baptism. And we thank you for sending us out into this world as your missionaries, for sending us out into this world as your disciples, for sending us out into this world as your apostles, those who are sent into this world to bring the good news. But first, Lord, before we're sent, we need to receive. We need to receive your grace. We need to receive your very essence, your very being, your Holy Spirit. So Lord, once again, pour out fresh among all of us, baptized and unbaptized, confirmed and not yet confirmed, pour out on all of us an abundance of your Holy Spirit. Because you promised you, Father, would give the Holy Spirit to all of those who ask for it. Jesus, you promised that your Father and ours would give the Holy Spirit to anyone who asks. And so, Father, in the name of Jesus, we're asking for that outpouring of the Holy Spirit upon our lives now and always. In Jesus' name we pray. Amen.

Dive **Deeper**

Recall the day of your confirmation. On that day, you were given the seven gifts of the Holy Spirit: wisdom, understanding, counsel, fortitude, knowledge, piety, and fear of the Lord. Write each gift down on paper or in a journal, and identify ways you could use them more intentionally this week.

Reflect on the **Faith**

- Sacred chrism is fragrant oil that is blessed by the bishop at the Chrism Mass, which occurs during Holy Week.

- When Confirmation is celebrated in the Eastern Church, there is more oil used on different parts of the body.

- The *Catechism* describes five effects of Confirmation, as well as an overall deepening of baptismal grace. The first effect is that we are further grounded in the relationship of son or daughter of God the Father.

- The second effect is that we are joined to Jesus more closely.

- The third effect is that the gifts of the Holy Spirit grow: wisdom, understanding, counsel, knowledge, piety, fortitude, and fear of the Lord.

- The fourth effect is that we are better united to the Church.

- The fifth effect is "a special strength of the Holy Spirit to spread and defend the faith by word and action as true witnesses of Christ" (CCC 1303).

- When we think that the Church or some of its members need to do better representing the Church, we need to remember that, as representatives in Christ's name, we all do.

- The gifts given to us through these sacraments, in their goodness, demand that we either use them or be rightfully ashamed for not doing so.

Take It to **Prayer**

Father in heaven, we give you praise, and we give you glory. We thank you for this sacrament of Confirmation. We thank you for the sacrament of this holy anointing where you pour out your Holy Spirit upon your children and send them forth and transform them. You increase the grace of the Holy Spirit. You increase the fruits, the gifts of the Holy Spirit inside each and every one of them. You open us up to a special strength to spread and defend the Faith by word and action. And we give you praise. We thank you so much for giving us the abundance of your grace in the rite of Confirmation. Help us to be open to that grace. Help us to open our hearts to allow you to move in our lives. But help us to be courageous. Help us to be generous in how we respond to your incredible gift of Confirmation. We make this prayer in the mighty name of Jesus Christ, our Lord. Amen.

Dive **Deeper**

THE SACRAMENT OF CONFIRMATION

Confirmation requires anointing with chrism on the forehead, as well as words that indicate that the person has been sealed with the Holy Spirit (see CCC 1300).

Reflect on the **Faith**

- "Every baptized person not yet confirmed can and should receive the sacrament of Confirmation" (CCC 1306).

- The custom in the Latin Church has been to separate the three sacraments of initiation over the course of a person's life: typically, Baptism at infancy, Holy Communion, and Confirmation when the person has reached the age of reason.

- The goal of preparing for Confirmation is helping the person to form a deeper relationship with Christ that is more filled with the power of the Holy Spirit.

- Even if you were not properly prepared to receive each of the sacraments of initiation at first, you can choose to root yourself in a deepened relationship with the Trinity as soon as you know of the opportunity for it.

- We must prepare with prayer and be free of mortal sin when we are confirmed so that we can receive the full effects of the sacrament.

- We are also asked to choose a spiritual sponsor for Confirmation. This should be someone who will help us grow.

- From the beginning of the Church, bishops conferred the sacrament of Confirmation.

- A priest can be permitted to confer the sacrament of Confirmation if necessary, in order that no one be deprived of the graces of God's sacraments in the hour of need.

Take It to **Prayer**

*Father in heaven, we call upon your name, and we give you praise and glory.
In the name of your Son, Jesus Christ, we ask you to please receive our thanks;
receive our praise. Thank you so much for this day. Thank you for bringing us to this
day. Lord God, we have done nothing to deserve life. We've done nothing to deserve
this day. And yet, here you are, once again, pouring out your goodness, pouring out
your gifts upon each and every one of us. As we draw breath, Lord God, every breath,
let every breath be a prayer of praise. Let every breath be a prayer of thanksgiving
to you. Let every heartbeat in our chests, Lord God—let it be for your glory
and a constant reminder how many times a minute of how good you are.
Let every heartbeat just declare and proclaim your goodness. May you be
praised and glorified. In Jesus' name we pray. Amen.*

Dive **Deeper**

If a candidate for Confirmation receives the sacrament without the proper intention, is the reception of the sacrament valid?

Confirmation is first and foremost God's confirmation of *his* choice of us. It is his gift of the Spirit, deepening the grace given to us in Baptism. Both Baptism and Confirmation are given only once because God seals us with the gift of the Holy Spirit—and he does not take back this gift.

As for the intention of the candidate, sometimes we can do a good act with mixed intentions; some of our reasons for choosing to do it may not be pure or spiritual but selfish (see CCC 1750–1754). So a teen may *choose* to be confirmed but out of a desire—*an intention*—to please his or her family. Even if one's intentions are mixed, it is nonetheless important to choose to do what is right. Much of the growth needed in the Christian life concerns the purification of our intentions and the development of our interior lives, learning to do the right thing for the right reason and to live from the grace that we have received.

Key reading: CCC 1302–1311, 1750–1754, 1792

Reflect on the **Faith**

- There is no person for whom Christ did not shed his blood, so he wants the whole world to know the Gospel and be Catholic.

- Jesus Christ established his Church to go out into the whole world, baptizing in the name of the Father, Son, and Holy Spirit, and making disciples. He did this because he desires that all men be saved, so what God has done in us does not stop with us.

- God gives us the sacrament of Confirmation to bring us close to him and to his Church and also to send us out to evangelize with the Church, pointing to Christ in all we say and do.

- "A candidate for Confirmation who has attained the age of reason must profess the faith, be in the state of grace, have the intention of receiving the sacrament, and be prepared to assume the role of disciple and witness to Christ" (CCC 1319).

- Going to Confession beforehand is highly recommended.

- We need to make sure to evaluate our intentions before Confirmation.

- If you are struggling but desire to be closer to the Lord, that is enough to be confirmed.

- Sacraments can never be forced on anybody.

- We can ask the Holy Spirit to fill our hearts and pour his graces into our lives now.

Take It to **Prayer**

Father in heaven, we give you praise. We give you glory, and we ask that you please send your Holy Spirit upon us. Send your Holy Spirit and pour out your love, your grace, your truth, your wisdom, your gifts so that our lives can bear fruit, the fruits of the Holy Spirit. Lord God, we consecrate this day to you, and we give it to you as an offering. We give it to you as a gift. We ask you to please simply receive this gift of this day—the gift of this day that you have given us. We give it back to you. Help us give it back to you in a way that honors you. Help us give it back to you as your gift to us and our gift to you. In Jesus' name we pray. Amen.

Dive **Deeper**

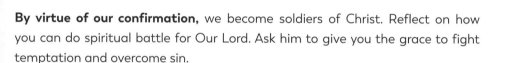

By virtue of our confirmation, we become soldiers of Christ. Reflect on how you can do spiritual battle for Our Lord. Ask him to give you the grace to fight temptation and overcome sin.

Reflect on the **Faith**

- "The holy Eucharist completes Christian initiation" (CCC 1322).

- Because Jesus offers his whole body, we are able to join in offering up that great sacrifice of the Eucharist—the sacrifice of the Son to the Father in the power of the Holy Spirit—since we have been fully initiated into his Body, the Church.

- The Eucharist is also a sign of unity. In fact, we only can be admitted to the Eucharist if we are in communion with the Church by being in communion with our bishops who are in union with the Holy Father.

- If the Eucharist is "a sacrament of love," it is also "a bond of charity" (CCC 1323). The more family members eat together, the more they have the opportunity to be bound to each other and recognize that they are called to love each other.

- The Paschal Mystery is the life, death, and resurrection of Jesus Christ, and the Eucharist is "a Paschal banquet 'in which Christ is consumed, the mind is filled with grace, and a pledge of future glory is given to us'" (CCC 1323).

- We say that "the Eucharist is 'the source and summit of the Christian life'" because it is the source of all grace, coming from the great sacrifice of the Son to the Father, and the ultimate goal for us all (CCC 1324).

- The Eucharist is not only a work of Christ: it *is* Christ.

Take It to **Prayer**

Father in heaven, we give you praise and glory. Thank you so much for bringing us to this day. Thank you so much for the gift of your Son in time— the gift of your Son, your only begotten Son, who gave himself for the sake of the world, who gave himself for us. We ask you to please, once again, renew in our hearts a love for you, a love for the gift of your Son, a love for the Eucharist. Lord God, let that love for you in the Eucharist dominate our lives. Let it become the center of all of our lives. Because all grace, all of your gifts—they lead us to the Eucharist, and all grace, all your gifts flow from the Eucharist. We thank you so much for this incredible gift. Thank you for this incredible day. Receive our thanks, receive our praise. You are good, you are God, and we love you. Amen.

Dive **Deeper**

THE LAST SUPPER BY JUAN DE JUANES

This image depicts our Lord's institution of the Eucharist on Holy Thursday, the night before his death. He gave us this sacrament "to perpetuate the sacrifice of the cross throughout the ages until he should come again" (CCC 1323).

Reflect on the **Faith**

- "Eucharist" is derived from the Greek *eucharistein*, referring to thanksgiving, and is connected to the Hebrew word for thanksgiving, *todah*. This highlights the profound sense of gratitude and thanksgiving present in the Eucharistic celebration.

- The rabbis taught that in the age of the Messiah, only one sacrifice would remain—the *todah* sacrifice, which corresponds to the Eucharistic sacrifice.

- The Eucharist is also known as the Lord's Supper and the Breaking of Bread, because Jesus established it during the Last Supper.

- Realizing who Jesus is "in the breaking of the bread" refers to the Eucharist in Jesus' appearance on the road to Emmaus after he has risen from the dead (see Luke 24:30–31, 35)

- The name "Eucharistic assembly" signifies that offering the Eucharist is not an individualistic act; it is a communal event that unites the faithful together as one Body in Christ.

- The name "Holy Mass" signifies that we are sent out to carry the grace of the Eucharist into the world. We get filled with the Holy Spirit and with Jesus' Body, Blood, Soul, and Divinity. And then we are sent out to bring that Body, Blood, Soul, and Divinity and to bring that Holy Spirit to the world.

- The Eucharist is described as a Holy Sacrifice, emphasizing that it is not a mere symbol but a true sacrifice, where Christ offers himself for our salvation.

- The Eucharist is the living presence of Christ, continuously offered to the Father through the Holy Spirit. It is the pinnacle of our worship—as baptized believers, we offer ourselves to God in union with Christ's perfect sacrifice.

- The Eucharist allows us to experience God's immense love in a profound and tangible way as we encounter the love of the Father through his Son.

Take It to **Prayer**

Father in heaven, thank you, Father. You have revealed your name to us. You've revealed the name of your Son, Jesus Christ our Lord, to us, and you've revealed the different ways in which we are called to consider the Eucharist. Lord God, when we begin to think that we know you, it's pretty clear that we only know something of you. Help us to know your heart in the depths, help us to know your heart as well as we know anyone's heart. Help us to know you even better than we know anyone.

As you continue to reveal yourself to us in your sacraments and your Scripture, here in the Eucharist, we ask that you please deepen our love for you, not just our knowledge. Broaden our love for you, not just what we know. And help us to allow you and your grace to transform our lives into living reflections of you, so that we can be walking tabernacles, so that we can be walking witnesses, apostles sent forth, because you have made us your children in Baptism. You have strengthened us with Confirmation. And you feed us, and you make us into yourself in this unique and mysterious way in the Holy Eucharist. Lord God, may you be praised and glorified. Hear our prayer, now and forever. In Jesus' name we pray. Amen.

Dive **Deeper**

THE SUPPER AT EMMAUS

This artwork by Michele Rapisardi shows the supper at Emmaus. After two of his disciples speak with Jesus on the road to Emmaus, they at last recognize the Lord "in the breaking of the bread," one of the names of the Holy Eucharist (Luke 24:35; see CCC 1329).

Reflect on the **Faith**

- The Eucharistic signs of bread and wine are gifts from the Lord, representing the produce of the earth and the Creator's generosity.

- Genesis 14:18 describes "Melchizedek king of Salem [who] brought out bread and wine; he was priest of God Most High." Melchizedek, offering this sacrifice on Mount Moriah, foreshadows Jesus, the King of Kings and great High Priest, offering himself as a sacrifice on Golgotha.

- Before the coming of Christ, the Jewish people presented bread and wine to God, with connections to the Passover and the miraculous gift of manna. All of this found fulfillment in Jesus.

- Jesus performed miracles with bread, multiplying it to give to thousands of people, which hinted at the Eucharist.

- Jesus' teaching on the Eucharist in John 6 caused disciples to abandon him, highlighting the very real difficulty and mystery of the Real Presence.

- "*To receive in faith the gift of his Eucharist is to receive the Lord himself*," and rejecting the Eucharist is rejecting the Lord (CCC 1336).

- The Eucharist is a profound gift of love from the Lord.

- The Eucharist fulfills the Jewish Passover, establishing the New Covenant in Jesus' blood. Every celebration of the Eucharist looks forward to heaven, allowing us to taste the love God has for us.

- God's love extends to each of us, regardless of weaknesses or failures. Attending Mass reminds us of his overwhelming love for us.

Take It to **Prayer**

Father in heaven, we give you praise and glory. We thank you so much. Thank you for the gift of your Son, Jesus Christ, the incarnate Word, two thousand years ago—given to us—eternally begotten of the Father, yet entering into time two millennia ago. We also thank you that you, Lord, Father in heaven, continue to send Jesus into our lives. You continue to give us the Body, Blood, Soul, and Divinity of your Son at every Mass. Lord God, we thank you, and we can never thank you enough. We praise you, and we can never praise you enough. We worship you, and we can never worship you the way you deserve. But we try. Jesus, you've asked us to do this in memory of you for the glory of the Father in the power of the Holy Spirit. Help us every time we approach the Mass. Help us to always approach with hearts that have been transformed by your grace, transformed by your Holy Spirit, and are able to worship you the way you deserve to be worshipped and loved. In Jesus' name we pray. Amen.

Dive **Deeper**

The Eucharist looks forward to heaven. Reflect upon how the Mass is a pure sacrifice that restores our brokenness. How has God restored you through Holy Communion?

Reflect on the **Faith**

- Jesus' command to "do this in remembrance of me" (Luke 22:21) goes beyond mere repetition or recalling to memory. It entails active participation in his actions and is crucial to the Christian Faith from the very beginning.

- Acts 2:42 highlights four essential aspects that marked the disciples' devotion: the apostles' teaching, fellowship, the breaking of the bread (the Eucharist), and prayers.

- These four markers define what it means to be a disciple of Jesus, emphasizing the importance of following the teachings of the Church, caring for others, participating in the Eucharist, and cultivating a life of prayer.

- Sunday became the day of Christian gathering and Eucharistic celebration because it marks the Lord's resurrection, and Christians meet on this day to participate in the Eucharist.

- St. Justin Martyr affirms that the Eucharist is not ordinary food but the true flesh and blood of Jesus Christ, to be received only by those who have faith, have received Baptism, and live according to Christ's teachings.

- The requirement of union with the Church and faith in the Real Presence of Christ in the Eucharist is not an act of cruelty but an act of love and protection. If someone does not believe in the Real Presence or they are not united to the Church or not living as Christ taught us, receiving the Body and Blood of Christ would place them in danger of receiving condemnation on themselves.

- In the Mass, the Scriptures are proclaimed and explained, and the bread is consecrated and shared.

- The story of the disciples on the road to Emmaus illustrates the two parts of the Mass, with Jesus revealing himself in the Scriptures during the Liturgy of the Word and in the breaking of the bread during the Liturgy of the Eucharist.

Take It to **Prayer**

Father in heaven, we give you praise and thanks. We ask you in the name of your Son, Jesus Christ, to receive our thanks. Receive our praise. Help us to receive you. Help us to receive your Son's gift, the gift of your Son himself in the Eucharist—Body, Blood, Soul, and Divinity—at every Mass we ever attend. Help us to participate in the worship of you, Father, as we continue to offer up the great once-for-all sacrifice of your Son to you in the power of the Holy Spirit that's given to us to participate in an unbloody way at every single Mass. Lord God, help us to put our whole heart, mind, soul, and strength into worship of you so that we can love you with our whole heart, mind, soul, and strength. For you are love. And you are God. It all comes from you. It all goes back to you. You are all in all. May you be praised forever, Father. We make this prayer in Jesus' name. Amen.

Dive **Deeper**

HOLY MASS

In every age, the Church's priests offer Holy Mass in obedience to Christ, who said to "do this in remembrance of me" (Luke 22:21; see CCC 1341).

Reflect on the **Faith**

- Christ brings us the Eucharist at each Mass.

- While paintings and drawings depict the visible elements of the Mass, they often fail to portray the heavenly hosts and the presence of Jesus Christ himself.

- In the Eucharist, Jesus is not only present Body, Blood, Soul, and Divinity, but he is also present as the great High Priest.

- Every baptized Christian has a great role to play in the Mass, exercising the kingdom and baptismal priesthood. You get to do this.

- The heart of religion is worship, and the heart of worship is sacrifice. The Mass involves both the reception of Holy Communion and the offering of the sacrifice, with the altar being the central place of sacrifice.

- The Eucharist is not just a meal but also a sacrifice, and participating in this sacrifice is an integral part of the Mass. Jesus commanded us to do this in his memory.

- While God's love is inclusive—Our Lord suffered and died for everyone, to redeem everyone—it is also exclusive. He has an exclusive claim on us, and we have to respond.

- Because of God's inclusive love, he wants all of us to be part of his family, to have unity with him and with each other. If we have not responded to his exclusive claim on our lives, we many not participate in the Eucharist.

- God's invitation for each person is to be fully united in the Catholic Church.

- You are made for the Eucharist. And the Church is not whole without you.

Take It to **Prayer**

Father in heaven, we give you praise and glory. We thank you for this day. We thank you for the gift of your Son, as always. Lord God, we can never thank you enough for the gift of your Son, Jesus Christ, our Lord; for the gift of your Holy Spirit that makes actual what your Son has made possible, your Holy Spirit that moves in the lives and the actions, the words of the priests, the words, actions, and lives of the people of God every time we come together and worship. Help us to worship you the way you deserve. Lord God, the next time we go to Mass, help us to worship you as if it is our first Mass, our last Mass, our only Mass. Help us to belong to you and to live lives worthy of you this day and every day. In Jesus' name we pray. Amen.

Dive **Deeper**

Does watching a Mass streamed in real time fulfill one's Sunday obligation?

Participating in Mass by simply viewing a video stream would not fulfill one's obligation to attend Mass on a Sunday or holy day of obligation. As the *Catechism* states, the need to go to Mass "is satisfied by assistance at a Mass which is celebrated anywhere in a Catholic rite either on the holy day or on the evening of the preceding day" (CCC 2180). The United States Conference of Catholic Bishops, in its "Guidelines for Televising the Liturgy," states that a televised Mass is not "a substitute for the Sunday Mass celebrated within a parish faith community each week." Catholics can be excused from the obligation to attend Mass only "for a serious reason (for example, illness, the care of infants)" (CCC 2181).

Key reading: CCC 2180–2181

Reflect on the **Faith**

- The story of Cain and Abel in Genesis 4 highlights the importance of worship as the heart of religion and sacrifice as the heart of worship. Abel's sacrifice was accepted; Cain's sacrifice was not, showing the significance of offering what God desires in worship to please him.

- In Exodus, God instructs Moses to tell Pharaoh to let his people go, not only for their freedom but also for the purpose of worshipping him (see Genesis 5:1).

- Moses' response to Pharaoh's offer to let the Israelites go to worship reveals the importance of giving God what he wants in worship, rather than presuming to know what he desires. (See Exodus 10:25–26).

- Jesus instituted the Eucharist, providing clear guidance on how God wants to be worshipped.

- The Eucharist is a sacrificial memorial of Christ's self-offering to the Father.

- Our active participation in the Mass matters to God. It is a response to his desire for our presence, engagement, and wholehearted worship.

- The sacrifice of the Eucharist goes beyond our individual participation.

- We acknowledge that all glory and honor belong to God and express our gratitude and adoration through the sacrificial worship made possible by Jesus' redemptive work.

- God invites, commands, and calls us to be present, engaged, and reverent during the Eucharistic celebration.

- The Eucharist is an extraordinary gift that surpasses our understanding.

Take It to **Prayer**

Father, we know that you love us. We know that you have given your own Son, so we can have life and have it to the full. We know what he has done for us in offering himself in sacrifice to you—a sacrifice of love, a sacrifice of praise, a sacrifice of thanksgiving. We know that that sacrifice has changed the course of every one of our lives because that sacrifice, the sacrifice of your Son, made it possible for us to have access to you. Help us to participate in this sacrifice, the sacrifice of the Mass, with our whole heart. Help us to participate in the sacrifice of the Mass as if every time we approach the Mass, we approach as if it's our first Mass, our last Mass, and our only Mass. In Jesus' name we pray. Amen.

Dive **Deeper**

CAIN AND ABEL

The story of Cain and Abel in the book of Genesis, pictured here, is a reminder of the importance of sacrifice in Catholic tradition (see CCC 1357).

Reflect on the **Faith**

- The "memorial" aspect of the Eucharistic sacrifice goes beyond a simple remembrance and is more like the Passover in the Old Covenant, where the Jewish people once again experience God's saving work.

- The celebration of the Passover recalls the deliverance of the Chosen People from slavery and death to a place of life and freedom.

- From the Last Supper to the Resurrection, the entirety of Christ's journey is one action of self-offering to the Father.

- The Eucharist is a "noun"—it is the Body and Blood of Christ. It is also a "verb"—it is the action of the sacrifice of Jesus offered to the Father.

- "The Eucharist is ... a sacrifice because it *re-presents* (makes present) the sacrifice of the cross" (CCC 1366).

- Our participation in the Mass contributes to the glorification of the Father and the sanctification of the world. It matters to God whether we are there or not. When we do not participate in the Mass, we do not utilize our kingdom priesthood, and the Father is just that much less glorified, and the world is just that much less sanctified.

- Remember, the Body of Christ is offered. And if you are a member of his Body, that means you are offered.

- The Mass allows us to participate fully by actively offering the sacrifice, as well as by joining our lives and experiences to Christ's sacrifice.

- Everything we go through can be offered and united to Christ's sacrifice, for the glory of the Father and the salvation of the world.

Take It to **Prayer**

Father in heaven, we thank you, and we praise you. We thank you for bringing us into your Body. Thank you for giving us your Body. And thank you so much for the sacrifice of your Body, Blood, Soul, and Divinity, for our salvation. Lord, without you, without you, we are lost. Without you, we are nothing. Without you, there is nothing. You are the foundation of all being. You are the foundation of all truth, of all love, of all goodness. Help us to participate in your goodness. Help us to cooperate with your goodness. Help us to live and walk in your truth. And help us to be signs of your love in this world to the people around us. Lord God, help us truly to be your Body as we walk this earth, to lift up those who are among us who have fallen, to bring light to those who walk in darkness, and to bring hope to those who are discouraged. Father, be with us now and give us your Holy Spirit. We make this prayer in the name of Jesus Christ, our Lord. Amen.

Dive **Deeper**

At Mass, we participate in the sacrifice on Calvary. Next time you go to Mass, imagine yourself at the foot of the Cross with Our Lady and St. John. In this meditation, offer prayers to unite yourself with Jesus on the Cross.

Reflect on the **Faith**

- The pope and bishops are mentioned in each Mass since they represent the oneness of the Catholic Church.

- We believe in the Real Presence of Jesus in the Eucharist, as stated in John 6 and the accounts of the Last Supper. There must be the ministerial priesthood in apostolic succession for a valid Eucharist.

- The Eucharistic sacrifice joins together all Catholics who are living now and also the souls in heaven.

- "In communion with and commemorating the Blessed Virgin Mary and all the saints, the Church offers the Eucharistic sacrifice. In the Eucharist the Church is as it were at the foot of the cross with Mary" (CCC 1370).

- The Church, the Body of Christ, also includes the holy souls in purgatory.

- Since the earliest times, the Church has believed in purgatory, a state of purification, and has offered prayers and the Mass for the holy souls in purgatory to aid in their journey toward complete purification.

- The Eucharistic sacrifice serves two essential purposes: giving glory to the Father and contributing to the sanctification and salvation of the world.

- The Mass provides an opportunity to remember and pray for our loved ones who have died, as it is a powerful means to express our love for them and our faith in Jesus Christ's victory over death.

- At their core, funerals are prayers for the deceased, acknowledging that not everyone goes straight to heaven. We may feel helpless after a loved one has died, but we can still pray for them and have Mass offered for them.

- Purgatory purifies our hearts from attachments and small loves so that we can fully love God with all our heart, mind, soul, and strength.

- We should pray for all the holy souls in purgatory.

Take It to **Prayer**

Father in heaven, we give you praise and glory and thank you. We thank you for your universal Church. We thank you for the Church that is visible, that we have a structure, that we are united with our bishop. We thank you that we are united with the Holy Father, our Pope, that you gave to us. Lord God, thank you for giving us this visible structure of the Church that we can point to, that we can look to, that we can hear from it, that we can be led and taught by. We also thank you, God, for the invisible Church, your invisible Body, that we cannot see but we do know is even more real than anything we can see: All the saints and angels in heaven that continually give you praise; we thank you and unite our prayers with their prayers. We thank you for all the souls in purgatory who by your great love are being purified at this very moment so that they can see you face-to-face for eternity. Lord God, may you be glorified. Please care for those—purify those souls in purgatory. Help them to become—to have hearts like yours so that they can see your face and experience your glory. Help us the same way, Lord God. Help us in that same way that purifies our hearts. Mend our broken hearts, strengthen us so that we can race towards you with your grace, with your help, with your love as our fuel. We make this prayer in the mighty name of Jesus Christ, our Lord. Amen.

Dive **Deeper**

ANGELS ADORING THE EUCHARIST

The painting shown here is a beautiful reminder that the Eucharistic sacrifice unites not only the members of the Church on earth but also the saints and angels (see CCC 1370).

Reflect on the **Faith**

- In the Holy Eucharist, Christ is present in a way that is different from the other ways he is present. "In the most blessed sacrament of the Eucharist 'the body and blood, together with the soul and divinity, of our Lord Jesus Christ and, therefore, *the whole Christ is truly, really, and substantially* contained" (CCC 1374).

- "This presence is called 'real' ... because it is ... a *substantial* presence by which Christ, God and man, makes himself wholly and entirely present" (CCC 1374).

- From the beginning, the meaning of the Eucharist was recognized when many disciples walked away after Jesus spoke about his flesh and blood as true food and drink.

- Church Fathers such as St. John Chrysostom and St. Ambrose emphasized the reality of the Eucharist as the true flesh and blood of Jesus Christ.

- The ability to "confect" the Eucharist is connected to the ministry and role of the priest, as expressed by St. John Chrysostom.

- The transformation in the Eucharist is called *transubstantiation,* where the "accidents" (appearance) of bread and wine remain the same, but the substance changes.

- Regardless of the size of the Communion Host we may receive, we receive the whole Christ.

Take It to **Prayer**

Father in heaven, we give you praise, and we thank you. We thank you for the gift of your Church, the gift of faith, hope, and love. We thank you for the gift of your Holy Spirit. We thank you for the gift of your Son. For you so loved the world that you gave your only Son so that everyone who believes in him may not perish but might have eternal life. And you've given us your Son to be our food in this miraculous, mysterious, incredible way. Help us to recognize him in the breaking of the bread. Help us to really, truly see who Jesus is as he comes to us on a regular basis, on a daily basis in the Eucharist. And help us to fall in love with him as you are in love with us. In Jesus' name we pray. Amen.

Dive **Deeper**

THE CONSECRATION

Through the words of consecration prayed by the priest, bread and wine are converted into the Body and Blood of Christ (see CCC 1375).

Reflect on the **Faith**

- The Eucharist is "truly, really, and substantially" the Body, Blood, Soul, and Divinity of Jesus Christ, the Son of God made man (CCC 1374).

- Worshipping the Eucharist includes bowing down before it in recognition of the divine presence.

- Some question this doctrine, saying that adoration is idolatry. If Catholic doctrine were wrong, worship of what appears to be bread and wine would be idolatry. However, Jesus said, "This is my body ... this is my blood" (Matthew 26:26, 28). We can trust the one who is Truth to tell us the truth.

- Catholics are not committing idolatry but instead are worshipping.

- The opportunity to be in God's presence and worship him is uniquely presented through the Eucharist.

- Worshipping Jesus in the Eucharist involves recognizing he is truly present even though we cannot perceive him with our five senses.

- St. Robert Bellarmine emphasized believing in Jesus' words about his Body and Blood in the Eucharist. Should we trust the opinions of others over the words of Christ? Of course not.

- St. John Paul II emphasized the "great need for Eucharistic worship" as "Jesus awaits us in this sacrament of love." He said, "Let us not refuse the time to go to meet him in adoration" (quoted in CCC 1380).

- Spending time in front of the Eucharist may not always result in a tangible transformation, but it holds great power and significance.

- The place where the Eucharist offered, the altar, is both the place of sacrifice and the place of the banquet, representing worship and communion with the Body and Blood of Christ.

Take It to **Prayer**

Father in heaven, thank you so much. We just give you praise today. We give you praise because you have given us everything. You have given us being. You've given us existence. You have given us breath. Lord God, every day we've ever lived, every heartbeat we've ever experienced, every thought we've had, Lord, has its origin in you. Let all of those—heartbeats and thoughts and days—let them all be directed towards your glory. Help us to love you with all of our heart, mind, soul, and strength. Help us to love you with everything we have. Help us to take care of our neighbors. You've given yourself to us in love. Help give ourselves back to you in love. And as you've shown us what it is to love without cost, we ask you to help us to love each other without cost, expecting nothing in return. Help us to give love for love. In Jesus' name we pray. Amen.

Dive **Deeper**

How can we as Catholics explain the Real Presence of Jesus in the Eucharist to others?

Some things exist only inside one's mind, such as thoughts. When the Church speaks of the "Real Presence" of Jesus in the Eucharist, though, it means something that exists outside of us—a presence that does not depend upon us.

While God is present in all that exists, upholding and sustaining it as its "cause," the Real Presence is *supremely* and *qualitatively* different. In the Eucharist, God is present "*substantially*," in the fullness of his Being (CCC 1374). Some non-Catholic Christians believe that Jesus is "spiritually" or "symbolically" present in communion but not "substantially" present. In contrast, the Real Presence signifies that Jesus is present, Body, Blood, Soul, and Divinity, in the Eucharist under the appearance of bread and wine (see CCC 1374). The appearances of bread and wine remain, but the substance—what it is—is completely changed. While we cannot begin to understand *how* this is the case, the Church wants us to know *that* it is.

Key readings: CCC 1373–1381

Reflect on the **Faith**

- The Eucharist is the source and summit of the Christian life, and all graces flow from it. We must get ourselves ready to receive the Eucharist and not approach it casually.

- If we have serious sins on our souls, we must abstain from receiving the Eucharist until we have gone to confession.

- Bishops and priests have a role in pointing out the need for reconciliation before receiving the Eucharist if someone is living in public and persistent grave sin.

- Our own state of soul and repentance should be the focus, rather than judging others.

- Humility and faith are expressed in what the centurion said in Matthew 8:8, "Lord, I am not worthy ..."

- A one-hour fast before receiving Holy Communion is obligatory in the Latin Church.

- If we have a grave sin and receive Holy Communion, we are eating and drinking condemnation upon ourselves, The Lord wants to set us free.

- We have to recognize our own sinfulness. We recognize the Lord's truth and beauty and goodness in the Eucharist, and we recognize that he still invites us to come to him. We need to be prepared by the sacrament of Reconciliation, by confession, but also remember that Christ wants us to draw near.

- The Church invites us to frequent reception of Holy Communion. We are obligated to receive Holy Communion yearly, but preferably we will receive more often.

- The Eucharist is both a sacrificial meal and a banquet, encompassing both elements.

- We should strive to recognize our sinfulness, prepare through confession, and approach the Eucharist with confidence, humility, and boldness.

Take It to **Prayer**

Father in heaven, we thank you. We give you praise and glory. You are the God who has given your Son, and your Son has given himself. You have both given your Holy Spirit to us as the one who makes actual and makes present what Jesus made possible. And so we ask you to please send, once again, your Holy Spirit into our lives, into our hearts. Send your Holy Spirit, the same Holy Spirit that is active and that unites us to you, the Holy Spirit that lives inside of us, the Holy Spirit that allows us to cry out, "Abba," Father. Send that Holy Spirit into our hearts in a new way so that we can always give you thanks and praise—the praise that you deserve, the thanks you deserve—so that we can give you the kind of hearts that you desire for us. Make our hearts like your heart. Help us to love what you love. Help us to hate what you hate and keep us far from all evil. Keep us far from all sin and help us grow as your saints. In Jesus' name we pray. Amen.

Dive **Deeper**

What should I say about receiving Communion to family members who are non-practicing Catholics?

Since this can be a difficult conversation, pray for the Holy Spirit to guide your words as well as the hearts of your family members. You will want to communicate several fundamental themes: (1) God desires everyone's happiness and wants us to come to receive him; (2) whatever is holding them back from trusting God and striving to be faithful to him can be overcome through his grace; and (3) the Eucharist is Jesus' loving gift of himself so that we can be in communion with him. (The quotation from St. John Eudes in CCC 1698 is a good reminder of the purpose of the Eucharist.)

Have a sincere conversation about faith. Speaking about the Eucharist and the aligning of our lives with Jesus in this sacrament naturally flows from this more general conversation. We should look and pray for this opportunity and remember that our own witness is often the main way in which family members are helped to come to receive Jesus as he should be received in the Eucharist— our reverence for Christ in the Real Presence, our times of Adoration, and our lives reflecting his grace.

Key reading: CCC 1384–1390, 1698

Reflect on the **Faith**

- Holy Communion deepens and strengthens our relationship with Christ, enhancing our connection with him and intensifying our spiritual bond.

- It helps to separate us from sin, acting as a cleansing agent that removes venial sins and guards us against future mortal sins.

- When approaching the Eucharist, we must have an openness to change, recognizing the transformative power of this sacrament and being willing to be shaped and molded by it.

- Our disposition toward the Eucharist should extend beyond mere ritualistic participation and embrace a genuine desire for transformation, conforming our lives to the example of Christ.

- Holy Communion goes beyond a mere symbolic act of consumption; it has the transformative effect of making us more like Christ.

- Receiving Holy Communion stimulates an increase in love within us, fortifying our capacity to love God and others, particularly when our love tends to wane amidst the challenges of everyday living.

- Holy Communion serves as a remedy for venial sins, cleansing away these lesser offenses and purifying our souls, providing a source of healing and restoration.

- It is important to recognize that Holy Communion is not a magical solution or a quick fix but rather a deepening of our relationship with Jesus, which empowers us to resist sin and grow in holiness.

- Recognizing the proper order of the sacraments and the need for Reconciliation before receiving Holy Communion ensures that we approach the Eucharist in a worthy manner and in accordance with Church teachings.

Take It to **Prayer**

Father in heaven, we praise you, and we glorify you. We thank you so much for this day. Thank you for bringing us to this day. Lord, you give us life. You give us your love. And you pour it out into our hearts in abundance without measure. Lord God, you do not ration your Holy Spirit, but you pour out your Spirit upon us and into our hearts, into our lives, to whatever degree we are willing and open to receive you. Please, help us become more willing to receive your love. Help us to become even more open to receive your grace now and always. In Jesus' name we pray. Amen.

Dive **Deeper**

If the Eucharist cleanses us of venial sins (CCC 1394), then why do we confess them?

Though venial sins are indeed forgiven when we receive the Holy Eucharist, confessing them in the sacrament of Reconciliation is beneficial because it "entails both God's forgiveness and reconciliation with the Church" (CCC 1440). Confession requires us to examine our sins as well as the occasions and habits that lead us to sin, which can help in our resolve to avoid them in the future. As the *Catechism* notes, confessing one's sins "even from a simply human point of view, frees us and facilitates our reconciliation with others. Through such an admission man looks squarely at the sins he is guilty of, takes responsibility for them, and thereby opens himself again to God and to the communion of the Church in order to make a new future possible" (CCC 1455). Furthermore, in receiving and fulfilling our penance, we make amends for the sins we have committed (CCC 1459–1460).

Key reading: CCC 1440, 1455, 1458–1460

Reflect on the **Faith**

- Holy Communion joins us in the Body of Christ, as highlighted by St. Paul's words in 1 Corinthians: "The bread which we break, is it not a participation in the body of Christ?" (quoted in CCC 1396).

- The act of receiving Holy Communion requires a genuine belief in the Real Presence of Jesus and unity with the Church.

- The conditions for receiving Holy Communion include Baptism, faith in Jesus as Lord, and unity with one's bishop.

- Catholics who are not in full communion with the Church, due to mortal sin or other irregularities, should not receive Holy Communion.

- Instead of compromising the truth, moments of division should be transformed into prayer for unity.

- The process of understanding and accepting Catholic beliefs, such as the Eucharist, can lead to genuine unity and conversion.

- The Eucharist also leads believers to care for the needy, as expressed by St. John Chrysostom. God feeds us and sets us free, and so we are called to go and care for others in the same way.

- The Eucharist is the sacrament of sacraments. It represents and brings about union.

- Let us pray for the unity of all Christians.

Take It to **Prayer**

Father in heaven, we give you praise. We thank you. Thank you for this day. Thank you for, once again, coming to meet us by the power of your Holy Spirit and the person of your Son, Jesus Christ. Thank you for speaking your Word to us, your Word made flesh—giving your Word to us, your Word made flesh, your only begotten Son, so that all those who believe in you might not perish but might have eternal life. Lord God, this day we pray for the unity of all Christians. We pray that one day, once again, all those who follow after Jesus may one day be united around the table, one day be united around the altar of the Lord. Lord God, we pray, right now, that what divides us as Christians may be overcome by what unites us as Christians. We pray that in your mercy and in your great will and your great providence, in the miracle that only you can render, that you bring unity once again to all those who profess faith in your Son, Jesus Christ. Make us one, as you are one. We make this prayer in the mighty name of Jesus Christ, our Lord. Amen.

Dive **Deeper**

Christ desires that we "may all be one" in the Catholic Church (John 17:21). Sadly, Christians are divided, yet we still have hope of uniting. Take time today to pray earnestly for the unity of all Christians.

Reflect on the **Faith**

- St. John Chrysostom emphasized the importance of showing mercy and sharing with others, as we partake in the Eucharist. He said, "You dishonor this table when you do not judge worthy of sharing your food someone judged worthy to take part in this meal" (quoted in CCC 1397).

- The Eucharist is meant to transform us, preparing us for God's heavenly presence and kingdom.

- If we do not cultivate hearts on this earth that long to be with Jesus, to give God worship, and to praise him, then will our hearts be ready to enter into heaven and to love God the way he has called us to love him?

- The Eucharist helps us grow in love.

- Jesus in the Eucharist is hidden from our eyes, just as Jesus' divinity was hidden during his earthly life. Jesus hides himself in the Eucharist so that we may approach him without fear or hesitation.

- While we do not see him with our eyes, there have been documented miracles that reveal the truth of the Real Presence.

- When receiving Holy Communion, we are receiving the very heart of God.

- Our invitation is to give our hearts to Jesus at every Mass.

- Through the Eucharist, heaven can begin now, as time and eternity intersect at the altar.

- The Mass is where heaven and earth unite, allowing us to experience the joy and love of God that will continue for all eternity.

Take It to **Prayer**

Father in heaven, we give you praise, every day. Every single day, Lord God, you give us as a gift. Every breath you give us as a gift. Every heartbeat you give us as a gift. Lord God, help us to not be blind to your gifts. Help us to not be deaf to your gifts or even numb to your presence and your blessings that are in our lives this day and every day. We ask you to please be with us and reveal yourself to us. Lord God, help us to love you the way you deserve to be loved. Help us to worship you the way you deserve to be worshipped. Help us to be the people that you've created and redeemed us to be. Help us to enter into the Eucharist in such a way that it's a foretaste of heavenly joy that awaits us. And we ask this, make this prayer in the mighty name of Jesus Christ, our Lord. Amen.

Dive **Deeper**

THE ADORATION OF THE MYSTIC LAMB
BY HUBERT AND JAN VAN EYCK

The famous Ghent Altarpiece, shown here, reminds us that every Mass is a foretaste of heaven (see CCC 1402).

Reflect on the **Faith**

- The belief in the Real Presence of Jesus in the Eucharist is rooted in his own words and the accounts in the Gospels and St. Paul's Letter to the Corinthians.

- God's desire to nourish humanity is evident from the beginning, seen in the provision of food in the Garden of Eden and in the wilderness for the Israelites.

- The Passover sacrifice and consumption of the lamb's flesh and blood prefigured the sacrifice and consumption of Jesus' Body and Blood for freedom and life.

- Jesus is called the Lamb of God who takes away the sins of the world. This is not simply because he is meek and gentle but because his passion parallels the sacrifice of the lambs in Jerusalem and his sacrifice is fulfilled at the Last Supper.

- Jesus acts through ordained priests who offer the Eucharistic sacrifice, regardless of their personal sins, and it is through them that the sacrament is brought to us.

- Proper preparation, including confession of mortal sins and being in full communion with the Church, is necessary before receiving the Eucharist in order to approach it worthily.

- The Eucharist leads to adoration, worship, and the reception of Jesus' heart while offering our hearts in return, fostering a deep communion with him.

- The Eucharist continually reveals the depths of God's presence and grace, providing nourishment and healing for body and soul.

- Participating in the Mass and receiving the Eucharist allows for ongoing encounters with God and the reception of his grace, shaping our lives and leading us closer to him.

Take It to **Prayer**

Father in heaven, we thank you. We thank you for the gift of your Son and the Eucharist. We thank you for all the gifts, all the sacraments you've given to us, all the sacraments of initiation—Baptism and Confirmation and Holy Communion. We ask you to please, on this last day of our reflection upon Holy Communion, the sacrament of sacraments—you open our hearts and open our minds so that the nuggets can stay with us, so that they're not merely pieces of data or articles of information but that they really, truly are seeds that are planted in our hearts and our minds that continue to grow, that don't leave us ever, but that we carry them with us, and they continue to bear fruit in our lives. Lord God, help this day not to be merely a day of information transfer, but a day truly of transformation. In Jesus' name we pray. Amen.

Dive **Deeper**

How many times can a person receive the Eucharist on a particular day?

Our union with Jesus in the reception of him in the Eucharist is interwoven with our devotion to him. For this reason, the reception of Holy Communion should not be separated from the celebration of the Mass. Since the Eucharist is the Body, Blood, Soul, and Divinity of Jesus, it is simply "enough" to receive it once a day. That said, there can be specific circumstances when we can receive more than once. As the 1983 Code of Canon Law states, "A person who has already received the Most Holy Eucharist can receive it a second time on the same day *only within the eucharistic celebration in which the person participates* (CIC 917; emphasis added). This would include at a wedding Mass. The Code of Canon Law also states, "Even if they have been nourished by holy communion on the same day, however, those in danger of death are strongly urged to receive communion again" (CIC 921).

Key reading: Code of Canon Law 917, 921

Reflect on the **Faith**

- Jesus is the healer both of our souls and our bodies, and he has given the Church the ability to carry on his mission of making us whole and of saving us from sin.

- The sacraments of healing—Reconciliation (penance) and the Anointing of the Sick—offer real healing for the soul and body.

- Our sins not only offend God but also injure the Church and our brothers and sisters.

- Confession is a sacrament of repentance and change of heart, acknowledging and praising the holiness of God and his mercy toward sinners.

- In the sacrament of Reconciliation, our sins are absolved and forgiven; it restores our relationship with God and the Church.

- The Church, through love, through leading the way, and through asking God's help, continually works for the repentance and reconciliation of sinners.

- Confession is a recognition of our need for forgiveness and a testament to God's mercy for us, who are sinners.

- The struggle against sin and the pursuit of holiness is a lifelong process that God continually calls us to.

- Concupiscence, our tendency toward sin, remains with us even after Baptism, but aided by Jesus' grace, we can strive for holiness.

- Even in the midst of our brokenness and sins, God always calls us to a life of sanctity and to live with him forever in heaven.

- The sacrament of Reconciliation is a cause for gratitude and excitement as it offers the opportunity for forgiveness, reconciliation, and the pursuit of holiness.

Take It to **Prayer**

Father in heaven, we give you praise and glory. Thank you so much for this day. Thank you for bringing us to day 195. We thank you not only for giving us new birth and regeneration in Baptism, but also giving us the healing, your healing, in the sacrament of Reconciliation, your healing in the Anointing of the Sick. Lord God, for as often as we wander, you pursue us. As often as we stray, you chase us down. We ask you to please, Lord God, be that hound of heaven. Be that hound of heaven that never ceases to chase after us. Be that hound of heaven that never ceases to call us back to you. Help us belong to you, body and soul. Help us give our minds to you. Help us to love you with everything we are. And when we fail to love you, bring us home and heal us. In Jesus' name we pray. Amen.

Dive **Deeper**

Does God still hear and respond to the prayers of one in a state of mortal sin?

St. Paul reminds us that Christ came to save us not because we were good and deserving but because we needed him, as we were caught in the nets of sin and death (see Romans 5:6–8). He writes, "Where sin increased, grace abounded all the more" (Romans 5:20). This does not mean that it is *good* to be in a state of sin but that God does not let go of us; he is always seeking our good and provides the grace needed to turn back to him. Our turning back to him, though, depends also on our free cooperation with his grace.

So we can say with confidence that God *always* hears our prayers offered in faith. One of the best-known prayers is the Jesus Prayer, which speaks of our sinful condition before the Lord: "Lord Jesus Christ, Son of God, have mercy on me, a sinner." Using an image from St. Augustine, the *Catechism* teaches that we should think of prayer as the gift God gives us when we truly realize that we are "beggars" before him and need to ask him for everything in our lives, including prayer (see CCC 2559).

Key reading: CCC 604, 2001–2002, 2559–2561, 2616–2617

Reflect on the **Faith**

- Whether baptized or not, all people are called to convert, to deny themselves, carry their cross, and follow Jesus.

- Conversion involves turning away from sin and being saved through believing in the Good News and being baptized.

- The Church continues to work to help people repent and change their ways.

- Conversion is a deep change of the heart and can happen at different moments in our lives.

- Inner repentance is a fundamental part of conversion and involves a change of heart.

- External actions like fasting are important, but they remain empty without interior conversion.

- Conversion entails rejecting sin and resolving to turn one's life around.

- Conversion leads to a recognition of the magnitude of God's love and a deep sorrow for sin.

- The goal of the Christian life is to become like Jesus and the Father, which requires turning away from sin.

- Conversion is a lifelong process, so patience is necessary but action should not be delayed.

- Take time to reflect on the sins that lead away from Jesus and renounce them in the name of Jesus.

- Prayer is essential in the uninterrupted task of conversion, and today's prayer can be to renounce specific sins in the name of Jesus.

Take It to **Prayer**

Father in heaven, we give you praise. We thank you. We give you glory. You are good. You are God, and you call us. You call us not just to be good, you call us to be like you. You don't just call us to say no to certain things in our lives. You call us to say no to our very selves. You call us to deny ourselves, to pick up our cross, and follow after you. Help us to have hearts that are like your heart. Help us to love what you love. Help us to hate what you hate. Help us to be like you. We ask this in the mighty name of Jesus Christ, our Lord. Amen.

Dive **Deeper**

Know that conversion is an ongoing process. How is God continually calling you to conversion? Do you reject sin and have a love of virtue?

Reflect on the **Faith**

- Conversion involves various ways of turning back to the Lord, starting with the three main forms of penance: fasting, praying, and giving alms.

- Today we will look at a list of things we can do that orient us more and more toward conversion, and all these things come from Scripture.

- All these things are oriented toward making our hearts more like Christ. God is the goal.

- We deny ourselves something we want when we fast, we talk with God in prayer, and we give alms to the people around us.

- Love, expressed through the action of charity, "covers a multitude of sins" and brings about effective change (CCC 1434).

- If we walk, run, swim, or exercise in other ways, our bodies will be transformed. Similarly, the aspects of conversion listed in the *Catechism* are ways we can exercise our souls.

- One of the reasons we have crucifixes is to remind us of God's love for us. The crucifix reminds us that when we are willing to carry our cross each day and follow Jesus, he is close to us.

- The Eucharist and the sacrament of Reconciliation are essential for "daily conversion," allowing us to be "fed and strengthened" (CCC 1436).

- Regardless of our past struggles or failures, the Father's love is ever present, and Jesus invites us to come back to the Father.

- As we turn away from sin and turn to the Lord, the Father rejoices over us and welcomes us home with love and joy.

Take It to **Prayer**

Father in heaven, we praise you. We glorify your name. We thank you for not giving up on us. We thank you for constantly, constantly calling us to turn from sin, to turn towards your heart, towards your love, towards your mercy, towards your grace. Help us, Lord, each day to become more and more like you, to become more and more like your Son, Jesus Christ, who has a heart that hates sin, a heart that loves you, a heart that loves us. Jesus has a heart that loves the poor and those others forget. God, give us a heart like his. Help us. Help us to hate what he hates. Help us to love what he loves. And help us to become like our Lord and Savior Jesus Christ. I make this prayer in the name of the Father, and of the Son, and of the Holy Spirit. Amen.

Dive **Deeper**

How do fasting and almsgiving contribute to the atonement for sins?

St. Paul VI addressed this question when he wrote: "External penitential practices are accompanied by an inner attitude of 'conversion,' that is to say of condemnation of and detachment from sin and of striving toward God ... One fasts or applies physical discipline to 'chastise one's own soul,' to 'humble oneself in the sight of his own God,' to 'turn one's face toward Jehovah,' to 'dispose oneself to prayer,' to 'understand' more intimately the things which are divine, or to prepare oneself for the encounter with God."[4]

Regarding interior penance, the *Catechism* notes, "Scripture and the Fathers insist above all on three forms, *fasting, prayer,* and *almsgiving,* which express conversion in relation to oneself, to God, and to others." In addition to prompting interior conversion, fasting and almsgiving can also help make satisfaction for, or atone for, the temporal punishment due to one's sins, particularly inasmuch as these acts of penance contribute to the purification of the sinner.

Key reading: CCC 1434, 1472–1473

Reflect on the **Faith**

- Sin is not determined by whether someone is hurt, but whether we have been disobedient to God's commandments.

- Sin is an act of choosing one's own will over God's will, rejecting his authority and love.

- Sin also causes disunity within the Church, the family of God and the Body of Christ.

- Baptism brings us into a relationship with God and the Church, and sin disrupts both relationships.

- Understanding the depth of our sin and its impact on our relationship with God and the Church is a grace.

- Being reconciled to God and being reconciled to the Church are both needed, requiring forgiveness and restoration.

- Only God forgives sins, but Jesus has extended the power to forgive to human beings. It is the ministry of the priest but the power of Jesus that forgives.

- The sacrament of Reconciliation is the work of forgiving and restoring entrusted to the Apostles and their successors.

- Forgiveness involves releasing the debt owed by the sinner, while reconciliation restores the relationship. We may forgive others without being reconciled, but God restores us with both forgiveness and reconciliation in the sacrament.

- The authority given to the Church in binding and loosing carries the power to bring into union with God or bar from union with God.

- Embracing the reality of reconciliation with the Church and God is essential, though it may be challenging.

Take It to **Prayer**

Father in heaven, we give you praise, and we thank you. We thank you for the fact that while we wander away from you, while we sin, while we say no to you, you never say no to us. You never reject us. You never stop calling us back to your heart. You never stop loving us. You always want us to receive your forgiveness. You always want to receive us back into your heart. Help us. Help us to—in our sins, to never stay away for long, to never stay far from you. But in our sin, we ask that you please break through with the power of your Spirit, break through with your voice of grace, your voice that calls us home, that calls us back to you. Help us always say yes to you, especially after we have wandered far away. Call us home today. Bring us back now. In Jesus' name we pray. Amen.

Dive **Deeper**

Pray through an examination of conscience. Is there anything that this brings to the surface? Take time to go to confession this week.

Reflect on the **Faith**

- The sacrament of Reconciliation is described as "the second plank [of salvation] after the shipwreck which is the loss of grace" through sin (CCC 1446).

- In the early Church, confession was sometimes reserved for certain major sins like murder, adultery, and apostasy.

- Strict discipline was practiced, including public acknowledgment of sin and extended periods of penance.

- In the 800s, priests from Ireland introduced private confession between the penitent and the priest.

- This emphasized God's mercy and grace alongside the awareness of the ugliness and awfulness of sin.

- The essential elements of the sacrament have remained the same throughout history.

- The priest's role includes granting absolution, assigning penance, praying for the person, and doing penance on his or her behalf.

- The prayer of absolution was updated in 2023 with slight changes in wording.

- Contrition is an essential part of confession and is "sorrow of the soul and detestation for the sin committed, together with the resolution not to sin again" (CCC 1451).

- Perfect contrition is contrition that "arises from a love by which God is loved above all else," while imperfect contrition is driven by more self-interested motives (CCC 1453).

- God receives even imperfect contrition and grants mercy to those who desire forgiveness.

Take It to **Prayer**

God in heaven, you are good, and you are love, and you call us back to yourself, constantly. You continue to offer us and all peoples of the world reconciliation. You offer us your forgiveness because you are not only just, you're merciful. You not only are good and fair, you also extend your grace to us. And grace that we do not deserve, but a grace that we do need. You give us your mercy. Lord God, help us to enter into your mercy. Help us, help us to allow your mercy to enter into us. And give us the grace today to—whatever it is that is our sin, whatever it is that's keeping us away from you—to say yes to your love, to say yes to your grace, and to say yes to mercy. Break our hearts. Break our hearts and make us contrite. Break our hearts and help us fall more and more in love with you. Let us, help us to hate sin and to love you. In Jesus' name we pray. Amen.

Dive **Deeper**

THE SACRAMENT OF RECONCILIATION

The sacrament of Penance and Reconciliation extends the mercy of God to the sinner through the instrumentality of the priest. In the sacrament we can turn back to God and receive divine grace again (see CCC 1446).

Reflect on the **Faith**

- Contrition is the starting point, characterized by being sorry for sin and desiring to turn back to the Lord.

- Confession is the expression of contrition and involves making our sins known.

- Confession of sins facilitates reconciliation and freedom in human relationships.

- God already knows our sins, but confession gives him access to our wounds and allows him to transform us with his mercy and forgiveness.

- The sin against the Holy Spirit is the refusal to allow God to forgive our sins.

- "Confession to a priest is an essential part of the sacrament of Penance," and "all mortal sins ... must be recounted ... in confession" (CCC 1456).

- To be mortal, a sin requires three elements: grave matter, knowledge of its gravity, and free choice to commit the sin.

- Ignorance can affect culpability for sin.

- Confessing all mortal sins is necessary for true reconciliation and forgiveness.

- Confession is a collaboration with God, where we join him in acknowledging our sins.

- Satisfaction involves righting the damage caused by sins, and it is an act of justice and restoration.

- Our sins are forgiven when we are absolved, but consequences of sin may still exist and require efforts to restore what was broken.

- The satisfaction we make for our sins is done with Christ.

Take It to **Prayer**

Father in heaven, we thank you. We thank you so much for this day. We thank you for leading us and walking us through these teachings of your holy Catholic Church that you established in Jesus Christ and have continued to guide by the power of the Holy Spirit. Please, Lord, help us today to, once again, approach your teaching, the teaching of your Church, not as simply more data gathering, not just simply as another, kind of, item of interest, something to learn, but something to penetrate our hearts and minds and transform the way we live. Lord God, let this be transformation. Let this be an opportunity for conversion. In this day particularly, I ask you to please move all the hearts of those who have been away from confession for a long time. Help all of us to bring our sins before you, to trust you, to trust your mercy, to trust your love, and to trust the grace of your sacrament. We make this prayer in the mighty name of Jesus Christ, our Lord. Amen.

Dive **Deeper**

Is it sinful to miss Mass on Sunday due to work or illness?

The Mass is God's supreme gift to us. In the Mass, Christ's sacrifice on the Cross is made freely present to us as an undeserved grace so that we can be united with him in this offering. As the *Catechism* reminds us, "The whole of God's work is a *blessing*" (CCC 1079), and it is "in the Church's liturgy [that] the divine blessing is fully revealed and communicated" (CCC 1082). Our worship, then, is the just and right response. The term "Sunday obligation" should be seen in this light. Any deliberate refusal of the gift God makes of himself in the Mass would be a refusal of the divine love that has given all for us.

There are circumstances, though, when we legitimately are not able to attend Mass—when we are ill or need to perform necessary work (e.g., the work of a medical professional). On such occasions, the Church encourages us to participate spiritually through prayer and Scripture reading, especially the readings of the day.

Key reading: CCC 1077–1083, 1328, 2180–2188

Reflect on the **Faith**

- A priest who hears confessions has authority and responsibility.

- Jesus is the one who heals and forgives, but he acts through the priest. In John 20:22–23, we read that Jesus came to the Apostles and "breathed on them, and said to them, 'Receive the Holy Spirit. If you forgive the sins of any, they are forgiven; if you retain the sins of any, they are retained.'"

- Every priest, as he acts *in persona Christi* (in the person of Christ), acts as an extension of the bishop.

- Excommunication can be seen in 1 Corinthians 5 when St. Paul directs the Corinthians to remove a man who is living in a very serious sin so he can realize he is not in God's grace. Excommunication is a very serious penalty, but it is meant to be oriented toward healing.

- A priest's life is meant to be defined by the ministry of mercy.

- A priest should unite his heart to the heart of the Good Shepherd, being faithful to Jesus and the Magisterium of the Church.

- A priest who hears confessions "must love the truth" (CCC 1466).

- Confession is a place of healing, love, restoration, and power.

- We are called to pray for priests that they can have the heart of Jesus and receive each person into the arms of the Father in the sacrament of Reconciliation.

Take It to **Prayer**

Father in heaven, we give you praise and glory. Thank you so much for bringing us here. Thank you for giving us your mercy and thank you for giving us the priesthood. Lord God, I thank you for every priest who has ever heard my confession. And I thank you for every priest who has ever been patient with me in confession and with all those who are listening. I thank you for every priest who has ever administered your mercy to all of us in our worst moments. Lord God, I ask you to please bless all those men, all those priests who have given their lives so that your mercy can touch our lives. I ask you to please bless them wherever they are right now. Lord God, I ask you to please be with those priests who have been mean in confession, have been cruel in confession, have been short, brief, hurt, or even worse in confession. I ask you to please heal them, heal their hearts. Help them become more like you. Help them be servants of your mercy not masters of forgiveness. Help us all to be patient with each other because, Lord, on our own none of us is enough. On our own all of us fail. And so we make this prayer in the mighty name of Jesus Christ. And we trust in you, Father, Son, and Holy Spirit. Amen.

Dive **Deeper**

When we encounter the mercy of Jesus, it changes our lives forever. To hear a beautiful story about God's mercy, watch the Ascension Presents YouTube video "Confession Is a Place of Victory."

Reflect on the **Faith**

- "The whole power of the sacrament of Penance consists in restoring us to God's grace and joining us with him in an intimate friendship" (CCC 1468).

- When we confess our sins, not only are we forgiven, but also our relationship with God is repaired.

- God's grace doesn't just bring us back to where we were. It elevates and perfects us even more.

- If getting forgiven makes us holier, why not keep sinning to become even holier? St. Paul addressed that. He basically said, "No way, don't do that." We should not abuse God's mercy.

- When we humbly come before the Lord in confession, we experience an abundance of mercy. Confession brings peace and interior comfort.

- The God we have offended, the Creator of everything, actually wants to be friends with us. He cares about us and what we do. This should be something we reflect on and pray about regularly.

- Confession also puts right our relationship in the Church. We are all connected, so when one member suffers or is healed, it affects us all.

- When we fall and come back to the Lord, we grow in humility.

- An indulgence "is a remission before God of the temporal punishment due to sins whose guilt has already been forgiven" (CCC 1471). It is like a fresh start, wiping away the consequences of past sins.

- Jesus entrusted the power to bind and loose to his Church, and indulgences are part of that authority.

- Confession and indulgences are about allowing God to love us as we are. They are about choosing God's mercy and grace, and they require our cooperation with God's grace and the Church's authority.

Take It to **Prayer**

Father in heaven, we thank you for this day. We thank you for the great sacrament of Reconciliation. We thank you for the mercy that comes to us through the ministry of your Church, through the ministry of your priests. We ask that you please draw us closer to your heart. Please reconcile us to yourself. Help us, especially those of us who have hardened hearts to you, to your mercy, to your grace, to your love, help us to have softened hearts that are open to your grace, hearts that are willing to race to you. Lord God, draw all of us to take the next opportunity to say yes to you in confession. Help us to be purified from all of our attachments to sin. In Jesus' name we pray. Amen.

Dive **Deeper**

THE RETURN OF THE PRODIGAL SON
BY POMPEO GIROLAMO BATONI

The return of the Prodigal Son is a fitting image for the soul reunited to God in Reconciliation, which brings us back to God and his Church (see CCC 1468–1469).

Reflect on the **Faith**

- We are not just individual Christians but part of a larger community.

- God's love for each of us is immense, and he also brings us into his Church.

- Our actions affect others within the communion of saints—those in heaven, purgatory, and on earth.

- There are four aspects to gaining an indulgence: (1) doing the action itself, for example, praying the Stations of the Cross or praying the Rosary; (2) receiving Holy Communion; (3) going to confession within a week or so of that action; and (4) interceding on behalf of the Holy Father.

- Some people have concerns about indulgences because they seem like buying grace, but purchasing spiritual goods is absolutely prohibited by the Church and by Scripture.

- Indulgences involve letting go of attachments to earthly things and growing in our relationship with the Lord.

- The Church believes in growing in holiness and cooperating with God's grace. God has given us his grace, but we must work with it to grow spiritually.

- The sacrament of Reconciliation is a powerful way to experience God's mercy and forgiveness.

- Reconciliation services can highlight our unity as a Church family.

- General absolution, where forgiveness is given to a group, is rare and reserved for specific urgent situations. It must be authorized by a bishop and should not be abused.

Take It to **Prayer**

Father in heaven, we praise you and glorify your name. We thank you so much. Again, let our time begin with praise. Let thanksgiving and praise go up first. Help us to praise you when we are thriving and when it's easy to forget you. Help us praise you when we are struggling and it's difficult to see you. Lord God, help us to praise you when we need your mercy. And help us to praise you when we have received your mercy. Help us in this day to walk in grace. Help us this day to recognize that we are not alone. We are surrounded by the great cloud of witnesses, the Church. And help us to take that next step, whatever that next step is, to grow closer and closer to you and your Sacred Heart, your merciful heart. In Jesus' name we pray. Amen.

Dive **Deeper**

PURGATORY

This image of purgatory reminds us that the souls there are part of the communion of saints, and thus our prayers and sacrifices can help remit their temporal punishment (see CCC 1479).

Reflect on the **Faith**

- The sacrament of Reconciliation exists because Jesus established it as a way for us to receive forgiveness and reconciliation.

- Jesus gave the authority to forgive sins to the Apostles, and this authority has been passed down to their successors.

- Our perspective on Confession reflects our hearts—pride or gratitude.

- Confession allows us to humbly surrender our sins and receive God's infinite mercy through the ministry of the priest and the Church.

- Hatred of sin is crucial, as there is no greater evil with more harmful results for individuals, the Church, and all humanity. Sin is worse than suffering or death.

- Conversion involves being sorry for sins, resolving not to sin again, and revealing sins to the priest.

- The sacrament of Reconciliation has six "spiritual effects": (1) "reconciliation with God by which the penitent recovers grace," (2) "reconciliation with the Church," (3) "remission of the eternal punishment incurred by mortal sins," (4) "remission, at least in part, of temporal punishments," (5) "peace and serenity of conscience, and spiritual consolation," and (6) "spiritual strength for the Christian battle" (CCC 1496).

- We may not always feel peace after confession, but it is a valuable gift, nonetheless.

- Confession makes us stronger as we fight sin, just like the Eucharist does.

- We should pray for God's help to be warriors against sin, asking him to be our shield.

Take It to **Prayer**

Father in heaven, we give you praise and glory. We thank you. We thank you for your love, your unstoppable and unfailing love. We thank you for your mercy that meets us in our misery. Lord God, we have mercenary hearts and you have a merciful heart. And we ask that you please meet us in our brokenness and meet us even in our resistance to grace, whether that resistance be anger or frustration, whether that resistance be self-condemnation or embarrassment, if that resistance is shame or is anger. Lord, God, I ask you to, please, meet every one of us wherever we are and bring us to your mercy, bring us to your grace, and bring us to your heart. We make this prayer in the mighty name of Jesus Christ, our Lord. Amen.

Dive **Deeper**

One of the conditions for mortal sin is to know that something is gravely sinful. Doesn't learning more about the Faith make it more likely to commit a mortal sin, then?

As the Catechism explains, "For a *sin* to be *mortal*, three conditions must together be met": (1) the action (or omission) must be "grave matter" (i.e., be objectively seriously sinful); (2) one must know that the action is gravely sinful; and (3) one must deliberately and fully consent to it (see CCC 1857).

Jesus, in his mercy, came to remind us that the light of truth is not our enemy. He called us to love the light, to come into the light and live in it. Those who choose to remain in darkness do so because they do not want their deeds to be seen. In the end, this refusal to come into the light is the result of the mistaken belief that God's truth will ruin their lives; it is lack of trust that God only wants what is good for us. This is the same lie the Serpent told Adam and Eve in the Garden, leading them to commit the first sin. But, as the *Catechism* insists, God is the fullness of loving truth (see CCC 214), and we only hurt ourselves by refusing to know—and live by—that truth.

Key reading: CCC 214–221, 391–392, 397, 1857–1860

Reflect on the **Faith**

- Our posture in the face of illness and suffering should be one of docility—being open to being taught and learning from the experience.

- The Church teaches us how to approach illness and suffering with the right posture, even when we feel bitter or resentful.

- The core of the sacrament of the Anointing of the Sick is the sacred anointing and prayer of the priests, as described in James 5.

- Sickness and pain have always been significant challenges in human life, making us aware of our weakness and mortality.

- In sickness, we can become selfish and refuse to accept God's will, or we can take the opportunity to grow and to seek God.

- In times of ill-health, we can gain clarity in recognizing the important things in life, and we can join ourselves with the suffering and death of Christ.

- Illness is connected to the brokenness caused by sin in the world, but not every personal illness is a direct result of personal sin.

- Jesus is the ultimate healer.

- Not everyone who came to Jesus was physically cured. Jesus does not remove sickness and suffering; instead, he redeems and transforms them.

- We are called to join our suffering, whether big or small, to the suffering of Christ, participating in the salvation of the world.

Take It to **Prayer**

Father in heaven, we thank you because you have sent your Son to heal us, not only to physically heal us; you sent your Holy Spirit to heal us, not only to physically heal us. You have sent your Holy Spirit, you have sent your Son to give us a deeper healing, a healing that no one else can give. You've sent your Son to give us a spiritual healing. You sent your Holy Spirit to reconcile us with you. You sent your Holy Spirit to kill the spiritual illness in the depths of our hearts and the depths of our souls. We ask you, God, this day, give us patience in suffering. Give us understanding. Help our hearts become softer, not more brittle, in the midst of sickness. Help our wills and our minds become more open to you and more inclined to you in the midst of our own pain and the pains of others. Help us all to grow in maturity and in trust in you in the midst of our suffering, not in despair and not in resentment in the midst of our suffering or the sufferings of others. But please, like you always do, meet us in our suffering. Be with us at this moment, at our best moments, at our worst moments, and at every moment. We ask this in the name of your Son, Jesus Christ, our Lord. Amen.

Dive **Deeper**

Through the sacrament of Reconciliation our relationship with God is restored to new life. Reflect upon God's abundant mercy and gentle heart. Take time to pray the Divine Mercy Chaplet today.

Reflect on the **Faith**

- Jesus' miracles of healing are not only a sign of God's love and care but also a sign that he is who he says he is—he is God.

- Our call to carry our crosses with Jesus transforms the way we see sickness.

- God may allow us to experience illness as a correction so we will change our lives, or because he wants us to grow, or because he wants to soften our hearts. He also may allow us to experience suffering because it is redemptive.

- St. John Paul II wrote in *Salvifici Doloris* that nothing is lacking in the sufferings of Christ, but Jesus extends to us a sliver of his Cross so that you and I can be co-workers in the mystery of his redemptive work in this world.

- Jesus wants us to share in his affliction as well as his glory, shaping our hearts to be more like his.

- While some people have the gift of healing, not everyone is physically cured, but all can unite their sufferings to Christ.

- Pain and suffering remind us of our finiteness and can be God's megaphone to awaken us from spiritual slumber.

- The Church reaches out to the sick through the sacrament of the Anointing of the Sick, which we see described in James chapter 5.

- The Anointing of the Sick is a powerful sacrament where the sick are anointed with holy oil for healing and forgiveness.

- Receiving or witnessing the Anointing of the Sick is a consoling and blessed experience.

- Priests who administer the Anointing of the Sick show selfless dedication, going to great lengths to be present for the sick. We should support them with our prayers.

Take It to **Prayer**

Father in heaven, we love you, and we know without a doubt that you love us. We know that whether you heal us or whether you are just present to us in the midst of our pain, in the midst of our suffering, we know that you love us. Lord God, for all the moments when it's difficult, difficult to acknowledge this, difficult to accept your love as it is, difficult to accept your will, O God, as often as it is hard to not be healed, we ask that you please come and meet us with your strength, and meet us with your grace. Help our hearts not to become hardened to you, but help our hearts to continue to melt in your presence. Help us always to trust you and help us to never stay afar from you, especially when we need you the most. In our woundedness, in our wickedness, in our suffering, and in our sickness be with us this day and every day. Help us choose you this day and every day. In Jesus' name we pray. Amen.

Dive **Deeper**

How does the notion of uniting your suffering with Jesus challenge your understanding of suffering? In what ways can suffering lead to spiritual growth and a deeper connection with Christ?

Reflect on the **Faith**

- The Anointing of the Sick was previously given to those about to die and called Extreme Unction or last rites. However, the sacrament is not only for the dying but for anyone "in danger of death from sickness or old age" (CCC 1514).

- Serious illnesses and surgery warrant receiving the Anointing of the Sick.

- The sacrament can be received again if the person gets better for a time but falls ill again with a serious condition.

- When there is a serious illness, it is important not to wait to call a priest, as some priests wish families had called sooner.

- Some families may hesitate to call a priest, fearing it would scare the sick person, but it is better to confront the seriousness of the illness to prepare spiritually.

- The Anointing of the Sick helps a person spiritually prepare and receive God's grace in facing their illness.

- The Anointing of the Sick is sometimes received along with confession and Holy Communion (Viaticum) to prepare the person for death.

- Viaticum is the Eucharist given as food for the passage from this life to the next.

- The Anointing of the Sick brings comfort and strength to those nearing the end of their earthly lives.

- The sacraments, including the Anointing of the Sick, are gifts of God's mercy and grace that bring us into his family and restore us to health.

Take It to **Prayer**

Father in heaven, we give you praise and glory. Thank you so much. Thank you so much for bringing us to this day. You call us to trust in you with our whole heart, mind, soul, and strength. You call us to love you with our whole heart, mind, soul, and strength. And so we do. We surrender our heart and entire lives to you because you are good. You are our Father, and you love us. We know that you do. And so we declare our trust in your love for us, in healing and outside of healing, and in abundance of life and in danger of imminent death. Lord God, we trust in you. Help us to trust you always. In Jesus' name we pray. Amen.

Dive **Deeper**

When should one receive the Anointing of the Sick?

One who is experiencing a serious illness, facing major surgery, or is infirm due to advanced age should receive the Anointing of the Sick. As the *Catechism* states, "The Anointing of the Sick 'is not a sacrament for those only who are at the point of death. Hence, as soon as anyone of the faithful begins to be in danger of death from sickness or old age, the fitting time for him to receive this sacrament has certainly already arrived'" (CCC 1514).

The effects of the Anointing of the Sick include a special grace of the Holy Spirit to fortify and encourage the person in his or her illness, joining with the sufferings of Christ on the Cross and offering up sufferings for the Church. In this sacrament, "the Church, in the communion of saints, intercedes for the benefit of the sick person," who is given grace to be ready to depart this life (CCC 1520–1523).

Key reading: CCC 1511, 1532

Reflect on the **Faith**

- The sacrament of Anointing of the Sick provides grace to fortify and encourage a person in the face of severe sickness or being elderly.

- This sacrament acknowledges the struggles and fears associated with death.

- The grace of Anointing of the Sick "renews trust and faith in God," protecting from "discouragement and anguish" (CCC 1520).

- Even in minor inconveniences like the common cold, we can reflect on our response to suffering and recognize the temptation to become bitter.

- In the Anointing of the Sick we pray not only for physical healing but also for deeper spiritual healing and forgiveness of sins.

- The sacrament enables us to join our suffering with Jesus Christ for the salvation of the world.

- Our suffering can be transformed into something meaningful through the power of Christ.

- We can offer our suffering for the well-being of the Church and recognize that we are not alone in our suffering.

- The Anointing of the Sick "fortifies" us like castle walls, providing strength "for the final struggles before entering the Father's house" (CCC 1523).

- The apostolic pardon, part of the Anointing of the Sick, is a powerful prayer that grants a plenary indulgence, removing the temporal consequences of sin.

- The apostolic pardon is a precious and incredible gift of God's grace that we can request for loved ones in danger of death.

Take It to **Prayer**

Father in heaven, thank you for this moment. Thank you for this day. We know that so many of our brothers and sisters who are part of this podcast—they, on this day, are experiencing a great trial. They're experiencing suffering. They're experiencing sickness. Lord, on this day, many of those who are listening to this podcast may themselves be in danger of death, at the moment of their deaths, or facing the death of someone they love. Because of that, we ask you, please, Lord God, be with us not only on our mountaintops, not only in our joys and our victories, be there in our failures, in our falls, be there in our sufferings and our weakness. Lord God, be there in our sickness and use it. Use our valleys. Use our falls. Use our weakness so that you may be glorified, that you may be known, that you may be loved. And then we can do our small part to carry a particle of your Cross for the salvation of the world. In Jesus' name we pray. Amen.

Dive **Deeper**

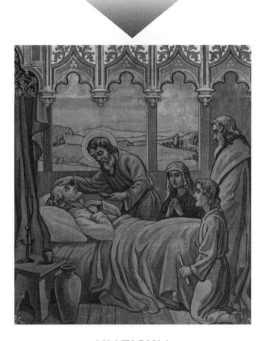

VIATICUM

The Church provides us with countless spiritual riches in preparation for death. This image shows one such gift, Viaticum, the Eucharist given as food for the journey (see CCC 1524).

Reflect on the **Faith**

- Our lives can serve as a practice for death.

- Often, we do not reflect deeply on death or the death of those close to us. Reflection is different from worrying, and it involves praying and meditating on our own death.

- The Church offers ways to prepare for death, such as making a daily examination of conscience. The examination helps us assess whether we are actively saying yes to God or being indifferent or rejecting him.

- Fridays and penitential seasons like Lent and Advent are opportunities for practicing detachment and freedom.

- By giving up things that bind us, we cultivate the readiness to let go and prepare for heaven.

- The Church provides these practices because it wants us to be ready for death.

- The Anointing of the Sick is a sacrament that offers particular graces for "the uniting of the sick person to the passion of Christ, for his own good and that of the whole Church" (CCC 1532).

- Anointing of the Sick brings "strengthening, peace, and courage," forgives sins, and sometimes even heals physically (CCC 1532).

- Above all, the sacrament prepares us "for passing over to eternal life" (CCC 1532).

- We should pray for those who have passed away and prepare our hearts for our own journey into eternal life.

Take It to **Prayer**

Father in heaven, we give you praise and glory. In the name of your Son, Jesus Christ, we ask you to please come and meet us in our need. Come and be with us in this moment. Fill our breath, our lungs, with your Holy Spirit. Fill us with your Holy Spirit. Fill our minds with your truth, with your clarity, with your goodness. Help us to say yes to you this moment and every moment of our lives. In Jesus' name we pray. Amen.

Dive **Deeper**

Reflect on the idea that the Anointing of the Sick serves a dual purpose: praying for healing while also preparing for death. How does this understanding reshape your perception of this sacrament?

Reflect on the **Faith**

- It is important to recognize the sacraments of Holy Orders and Matrimony as gifts from Jesus through his Church, even if we have had negative personal experiences associated with them.

- Holy Orders and Matrimony "are directed towards the salvation of others," not solely for the person's own holiness (CCC 1534).

- They are vocations of discipleship and serving people.

- Baptism, Confirmation, and the Holy Eucharist fully initiate us into Christ's Church and are essential.

- Holy Orders and Matrimony are gifts that allow us to live out our call to holiness and mission.

- Resentment should be avoided, and we should embrace the gift of each sacrament.

- Holy Orders consecrates individual men to serve the Church.

- Matrimony sets apart spouses to carry out their responsibilities in a way of life that is worthy of respect.

- Holy Orders "includes three degrees: episcopate, presbyterate, and diaconate" (CCC 1536). This refers to bishops, priests, and deacons.

- Ordination is not merely a "designation" but a passing on of the "sacred power" of Jesus Christ, enabling priests, deacons, and bishops to perform their ordained roles (CCC 1538).

Take It to **Prayer**

Father in heaven, we give you praise. Thank you so much for this gift. Thank you for this day. Thank you for this chapter three, this last section on the sacraments. And thank you for the gift of Matrimony. Thank you for the gift of marriage and family. Thank you for the gift of Holy Orders. Thank you for our own moms and dads. Thank you for those people among us who are married and live out their vows as best they can in the power of your grace. We thank you for our bishop. Thank you for the priests around us. Thank you for the deacons that serve in your Church. We ask you to please give them the grace that they need to be faithful to their vows, to live out their vows each day, Lord God, and give us—wherever a state of life we're in, wherever we are right now, we ask you to please give us the grace to live out our promises, to live out the consecration we've received from you no matter what vocation we are in now. Lord God, we know that when we were baptized you made us your sons and daughters. And that is at the heart of everything. Our primary call is to be your saints, to live like your sons and daughters because you have made us your adopted sons and daughters. Help us this day and every day to give you glory by living as you would live and by loving as you would love. In Jesus' name we pray. Amen.

Dive **Deeper**

Consider the significance of the promises of poverty, chastity, and obedience in religious life. How do these vows contribute to a deeper commitment to God and the Church? Take time today to pray for all religious brothers or sisters.

Reflect on the **Faith**

- In the very beginning, Cain and Abel are described in the first chapters of Genesis offering sacrifices.

- Melchizedek, a mysterious priest and king, appears in Genesis and offers a sacrifice of bread and wine (see Genesis 14:18).

- Abram encounters Melchizedek and gives him "a tenth of everything" (see Genesis 14:19–20).

- Melchizedek's priesthood is mentioned in Psalm 110:4 and the letter to the Hebrews (see Hebrews 5–7).

- Originally, fathers served as priests in their families, but this changed after the incident with the golden calf.

- The Levitical priesthood was established, and only priests from the tribe of Levi could serve.

- In the New Covenant, priests are referred to as fathers and are joined to Jesus' priesthood.

- Priests "act on behalf of men in relation to God, to offer gifts and sacrifices for sins" (CCC 1539).

- The priesthood of Jesus fulfills the prefigurations of fatherhood, Melchizedek's priesthood, and Levitical priesthood.

- The sacrifice of the Holy Eucharist re-presents the one sacrifice of Jesus at every Mass.

- Jesus is the one, great High Priest, and Catholic priests share in his priesthood.

- All baptized persons share in the priesthood of Jesus in a unique way as part of the kingdom priesthood.

- The more we exercise our priesthood, the more we make Jesus' priesthood present and glorify God.

Take It to **Prayer**

Father in heaven, we thank you and give you praise. We ask that you please send your Holy Spirit to bless us. Send your Holy Spirit to bless our local bishop. Send your Holy Spirit to bless our universal bishop, the pope. We ask you to send your Holy Spirit to bless the priest who baptized us, every priest who's ever heard our confession and fed us with the Eucharist, every priest who's ever given us counsel, every deacon who's ever served in our parishes and served our families and served us individually. We ask you to please, in this moment, to bless all those priests who have died, who have gone before us. Bring them into your presence. Purify them with your love so that they may dwell in your presence for all eternity. And we ask you to please bless us, Father. In the name of your Son, Jesus Christ, by the power of your Holy Spirit, help us to be holy. Help us to be yours. Help us to love the way you love. In Jesus' name we pray. Amen.

Dive **Deeper**

Jesus Christ is the one true priest. However, each priest participates in that one true priesthood. Take time today to pray for the priests in your life and thank them for their sacrifice.

Reflect on the **Faith**

- The faithful can exercise their part in the priesthood "through their participation, each according to his own vocation, in Christ's mission as priest, prophet, and king" (CCC 1546).

- Any suffering, work, and rejoicing can be united to that of Jesus, and when we worship him at the Mass, we can unite to his offering of self to the Father as well—but in a different way than a priest or bishop can.

- Although all believers share in the priesthood of Jesus, only those in the ministerial priesthood (bishops and priests) are able to act in the person of Christ.

- Dr. Leonard Sax writes in his book *Boys Adrift* that the primary two versions of flawed masculine ideals in the West are "the slacker dude" or "the bully," and both types exhibit an abuse of strength (either through failing to use masculine strength or through using it for selfish domination).

- Jesus is the prime example of unconquerable authority and power, and he puts it to use for the service of those around him, modeling what it is to be a good man.

- Just as the failings of a father can be devastating to his family, those of the priest can be equally so for the family of the Church.

- There is a weight put on priests to live up to their call and take care of their spiritual children, as they have, in some ways, a higher capacity to lead others into sin through their own sins. This is why they need to follow the example of Christ.

Take It to **Prayer**

Father in heaven, in the name of Jesus, in the power of your Holy Spirit, we present ourselves before you, and we ask that you please bless this time. Bless this time that we just hear these words of the Catechism. Bless this time that we come together in this virtual, and somewhat divided, and strange, and new way. But bless this time that we can actually be united as a Church, that we can be united as followers of your Son, Jesus, that we can be united by our common priesthood, the priesthood of all believers, and be united by the ministerial priests who have served us. Lord God, I pray that you please bless those ministerial priests. Bless them in their weakness. Bless them in their need for you. Bless them in their need for forgiveness, in their need for reconciliation. Bless them in their struggles. Bless every priest this day. Make them holy. Make them like you. In Jesus' name we pray. Amen.

Dive **Deeper**

We are all called to live priestly lives by virtue of our baptism. Make a small sacrifice today as a "kingdom priest," either by fasting, almsgiving, or prayer.

Reflect on the **Faith**

- The role of deacon was instituted to support bishops and priests.

- The entire tribe of Levi was called to serve at the altar. Those of the household of Aaron were priests, who would offer the sacrifice, while other Levites had different roles such as caring for the vessels or the tent.

- Even the Old Covenant priesthood was held in different degrees, and we see how the Levitical priesthood is fulfilled in the New Covenant priesthood that is established and bestowed upon the Church by Jesus.

- St. Ignatius of Antioch said, "Let everyone revere the deacons as Jesus Christ, the bishop as the image of the Father, and the presbyters as the senate of God and the assembly of the apostles. For without them one cannot speak of the Church" (quoted in CCC 1554).

- Without the priesthood, the Church could not have the Eucharist.

- Bishops make holy by bringing the people of God to God and vice versa; they instruct by clearly communicating the Word and the mission attached to it; and they govern through the their leadership in their own diocese.

- Bishops have an obligation to this trifold office, for the sake of the souls specifically entrusted to them. A bishop is responsible for every soul in his diocese—not only those who are Catholic.

- All who have said yes to a vocation that entails being responsible for other souls—such as teachers or parents, as well as priests and bishops—are liable to a greater judgment, so we must pray for them.

Take It to **Prayer**

Father in heaven, we give you praise and glory. Thank you. Thank you so much for bringing us to this day. Thank you for bringing us into your Church and for giving us the gift of Holy Orders. Thank you for giving us the gift of our local bishop and the universal bishop, our Holy Father, the pope. We ask that you please, on this day, please bless this man in a powerful and unique way. You've called him to serve. You've called him to participate fully—as fully as possible—in your great priesthood, your high priesthood. Please, preserve and protect him. Give him zeal and love. Lord God, make up for what he lacks, and give him every good gift so that he can teach, sanctify, and govern your Church as you would teach, sanctify, and govern your Church. We pray for him and all bishops in Jesus' name. Amen.

Dive **Deeper**

How are bishops chosen in the Church?

The first successors of the Apostles were chosen from among "proven men" (CCC 861). Throughout the early centuries of the Church, bishops were often elected by the clergy of a region or diocese, usually from among its own priests. In our own day, a process is followed in which the pope approves the selection of each bishop, based on the recommendation of the Vatican's Congregation for Bishops, whose members seek to gain knowledge about a particular candidate from those who can answer the question, "Is this a 'proven' man?"

The bishops of the particular region or nation will gather and discuss names of worthy men to be sent on to the *nuncio*, the pope's representative in a particular place. From these enquiries, three names are sent to the Congregation for Bishops. It is usually from among these that a man is chosen for ordination to the episcopacy. The chosen priest must freely accept to be ordained a bishop, of course; he always has the option to decline, though this is rare.

Key reading: CCC 861–862, 874–879

Reflect on the **Faith**

- Just as with the episcopacy, the presbyterate is called to participate in the trifold office of making holy, instructing, and governing—in imitation of Christ's trifold office of priest, prophet, and King.

- Priests are fellow workers with the bishops, forming a unique kind of brotherhood to serve the Church for the glory of God the Father.

- Jesus wants all of us to be holy by coming into contact with him, and ever since his time on earth, he has sent bishops and priests into the world to extend and continue his mission.

- Priests "act in the person of Christ the head" (*in persona Christi capitis*) to their own designated degree (CCC 1563).

- The height of a priest's sacred role comes through the sacrifice of the Mass in consecrating the Eucharist.

- The heart of the priesthood is the priestly heart of Jesus offering himself to the Father in the power of the Holy Spirit. The priesthood is empowered by the daily celebration of the Mass.

- A priest must be in good standing with his bishop in order to celebrate the Mass because of his promise, made when he is ordained, to be obedient to his bishop. When the priest makes this promise, the bishop embraces him, signifying his acknowledgment of him as a brother.

- There is a definite hierarchy in the Church, but even bishops and priests work together, and lay people have their own share of this priestly ministry. Jesus himself calls us friends, while we owe him our love and obedience.

Take It to **Prayer**

Father in heaven, thank you. Thank you for bringing us to this day. Thank you for giving us the gift of your grace. Thank you for continuing to bind up the weak. Thank you for continuing to heal our wounds. Thank you for continuing to forgive our sins. Lord God, thank you for continuing to give us yourself in the Eucharist, pouring out your Holy Spirit upon us. Whenever we pray, whenever we ask you, Father, for your Holy Spirit, you hear the prayer of your children, and you respond with love because you are a good Father. We ask you, in this day, when we talk about priests, we ask you to please help these priests be good fathers. Help these priests be men after your own heart. Help them to govern, to teach, to sanctify in the way that you would. And we ask you to please, please bless our local priests. Make them holy. Help them where they need help. Strengthen them where they need strengthening. Heal them where they need healing. Forgive them of all their sins. And, Lord God, help them to be the kind of men that we need. Help them to be the priests that we need them to be. In Jesus' name we pray. Amen.

Dive **Deeper**

What is the difference between a diocesan priest and a religious priest?

A diocesan (or "secular") priest is ordained by the bishop of a particular diocese to minister within its territory. As assigned by their bishop, diocesan priests usually serve as pastors or assistant pastors of parishes, though some also serve in other roles, such as teaching or directing various diocesan offices. All diocesan priests make a promise of obedience to their bishop. In the Roman rite of the Church, they also make a promise of celibacy. Unlike religious priests, they do not take solemn vows or live in community.

A religious priest is ordained as a member of a particular religious order (e.g., Franciscans, Dominicans, or Jesuits), in which he has made perpetual vows of poverty, chastity, and obedience prior to his ordination. Religious priests live according to the rule of their particular order, live in community, and serve in a variety of ministries.

Key reading: CCC 1567–1568, 1579

Reflect on the **Faith**

- After bishops and priests, deacons are the third tier within the sacrament of Holy Orders, and they are ordained to serve.

- "It is the task of deacons to assist the bishop and priests" at the altar for the Mass and "in the distribution of Holy Communion" (CCC 1570).

- A deacon's role also includes "assisting at and blessing marriages," reading the Gospel at Mass, giving homilies, "presiding over funerals," and generally doing charitable works (CCC 1570).

- We read in the Acts of the Apostles that when the diaconate was instated, the Apostles had a need for help with physical acts of service for the people while they themselves preached the Word.

- The Apostles chose seven men, laid their hands on them, and consecrated them to do this ministry.

- The "*permanent diaconate*," where deacons remain deacons rather than later being ordained as priests, was always in place in the East but has been reinstated in the West as well (CCC 1571).

- The importance of ordination warrants the presence of the entire diocesan assembly.

- There are two elements to "the *essential rite* of the sacrament of Holy Orders": the laying on of hands by the bishop on the person being ordained and "the bishop's specific consecratory prayer asking God" to give the man the graces he needs to carry out his calling (CCC 1573).

Take It to **Prayer**

Father in heaven, in the name of Jesus Christ, your Son, I ask you to please send your Holy Spirit upon us. Remind us of who you are. Remind us of your love. Remind us of your goodness so that we can trust you even more fully today. Help us to renew our faith, hope, and love in you. Those gifts of faith, hope, and love are truly graces from you. Lord God, pour them out upon us. Help us to say yes and respond to them in a powerful way, and never let us be separated from you. In Jesus' name we pray. Amen.

Dive **Deeper**

Why isn't a married permanent deacon allowed to remarry following the death of his wife?

Many Catholics are surprised to learn that a married permanent deacon is required to remain celibate if his wife passes away. In the history of the Church, there was a time when married men were admitted to the priesthood, but priests were not allowed to get married following ordination. The commitment of a permanent deacon to a life of celibacy following the death of his spouse follows in this tradition. Like bishops and priests, deacons are ordained to the sacrament of Holy Orders, and thus they are set apart for sacred ministry. A deacon, then, is not an important layperson who merely assists a priest at Mass; he has received an indelible spiritual character by virtue of his ordination.

Key reading: CCC 1583

Reflect on the **Faith**

- The *Catechism* states, "Only a baptized man (*vir*) validly receives sacred ordination" (CCC 1577). Regardless of an individual bishop's opinion regarding the ordination of women being possible, the Church cannot allow it.

- Jesus himself instituted the sacraments, so it never comes down to how we would choose for any of them to be celebrated validly. For Holy Orders, "the Lord Jesus chose men" exclusively (CCC 1577).

- Sometimes people suggest that Jesus chose men for the priesthood because he was a product of his culture and would not have singled out any women, but Jesus was known to raise up the dignity of women.

- The Church never says that men are better than women but rather consistently acknowledges that men and women are equal in dignity and equal heirs to grace. This distinction has been lost in our culture in so many ways.

- People in non-Christian cultures in the past might have thought women were inferior, but Christianity does not adopt that view.

- The priesthood has been particularly connected to fatherhood since its origin in the Old Covenant. In the Jewish worldview, the father was the priest of the family; Jesus is the fulfillment of the priesthood in the New Covenant.

- In many communities, religious sisters have been the ones to establish the most important organizations and ministries, so they clearly have a lot of capability and influence within the Church.

- It may seem unjust that women cannot be ordained, but the true injustice would be to go against what Jesus established.

- Jesus Christ gave us the priesthood as an image of his own self-offering and the fatherhood of God.

Take It to **Prayer**

Father in heaven, we ask you to please, in the name of your Son, Jesus Christ, send us your Holy Spirit, a spirit of wisdom, a spirit of knowledge, a spirit of understanding. Give us a spirit of docility, a spirit of being able to be taught. Give us a teachability, Lord God, that guides us when we don't understand, that guides us when we have questions, that guides us when we struggle. We ask you, Lord God, to give us minds that are quick, minds that are sharp. We ask you to give us minds that are willing to be led but also willing to ask questions. Lord God, give us minds that are willing to seek the truth and to hold onto the truth when we find it, wherever we find it. You are the source of all truth. You're the source of all goodness. You are the source of all grace. We ask you to give us your grace. Lead us to your truth. Help us to live goodness. In Jesus' name we pray. Amen.

Dive **Deeper**

The Church has handed down the teaching from the Apostles that Holy Orders can only be conferred upon baptized men. Watch the Ascension Presents YouTube video from Fr. Josh Johnson about female ordination called "Can Women Be Ordained Priests in the Catholic Church?" to learn more.

Reflect on the **Faith**

- Any man ordained a priest through the sacrament of Holy Orders receives a particular grace from the Holy Spirit oriented to serving the Church for Christ.

- Like Baptism and Confirmation, Holy Orders places a permanent mark upon the soul of the recipient, so the sacrament cannot be given twice or removed.

- We can never be worthy of any of the sacraments, so failing to live up to them perfectly is inevitable. It is essential to note that Jesus confers the grace of the sacraments through the priest, so a priest's flaws cannot alter what Jesus bestows.

- Each bishop in particular is given the gift of being a strong leader for his flock.

- There is a prayer for ordination that asks the Lord to pour out the Holy Spirit on the priest that he may fittingly offer sacrifice and be rewarded by Christ at the end of his life.

- Every one of us, regardless of vocation, longs to hear God say at the hour of death, "Well done, my good and faithful servant."

- Holiness is dependent on our response to God's call with love. St. John Vianney's words, "the Priesthood is the love of the heart of Jesus," acknowledge that men called to be priests are also holy only to the extent of their love and how it can imitate Christ's (CCC 1589).

Take It to **Prayer**

Father in heaven, we give you praise and glory. We thank you so much for giving us yourself, for giving us your Son, for giving us your love, and giving us access to your heart. Father in heaven, help us to love you with hearts that are undivided. Help us to follow you with wills that are undivided. Help us to be able to focus on you with a mind that's undivided, and help us belong to you, united in love for you, this day and every day. We make this prayer in the mighty name of Jesus Christ, our Lord. Amen.

Dive **Deeper**

CHRIST WASHING THE DISCIPLES' FEET

Jesus' act of washing his disciples' feet is a potent reminder that Holy Orders is a sacrament of sacrifice and service. The priestly office requires constant turning to Christ (see CCC 1589).

Reflect on the **Faith**

- From the first as he called the people of Israel, God desired for them to be a priestly people.

- The story of the golden calf tells us how the fathers of that community lost their priesthood, which is why the priesthood was given to the tribe of Levi.

- The priesthoods of Levi and of Melchizedek recognize the necessary role of a mediator to go to God on behalf of the people and respond to them with his messages, and this role is fulfilled by Jesus.

- God can communicate directly to the people themselves, but he has called certain people to act uniquely as his ambassadors, offering sacrifice to the Lord on behalf of the people and bringing back to them God's grace.

- God calls ordinary men to be priests, just as he calls ordinary men and women to marriage. They have ordinary hearts that are incapable of loving perfectly, but broken people can be representatives of God.

- Every one of us is called to a vocation so that we might serve. In pouring our lives out, we have the opportunity to become more and more like Jesus.

- Husbands and wives pour their lives out to each other in love for God for the salvation of the world, and priests pour their lives out to the Father in love for the sake of the Body of Christ.

- For anyone who has not yet been called to a specific vocation and is not sure if he or she will be called, you are not insignificant to the Lord. He can also help you to rejoice in the gifts that others receive.

Take It to **Prayer**

Father in heaven, we praise you and give you glory. We thank you so much. We ask that you please hear our prayer. We ask that you not only fill us right now in this moment with your Holy Spirit, a Spirit of wisdom, of insight, a Spirit of counsel and of knowledge, a Spirit of fear of the Lord, a Spirit that recognizes your gifts—the natural gifts you give to us each day with a sunrise, the natural gift you give to us each day of a heart in our chest that beats and breath in our lungs, but also the supernatural gifts that you've given to us through this grace of your sacraments, through the grace of your Church. Thank you for giving us the holy priesthood. Thank you for giving us Holy Orders. Thank you for our bishop and for our pastor. Thank you for our deacons who've served in the Church. Lord God, we ask you to please increase the number of men you're calling to serve your Church as priests and deacons. We ask you to please increase also religious communities, religious sisters, and religious brothers. Help all these vocations to abound in your grace. Continuing today, we're praying also for those who are called to holy Matrimony, recognizing that, Lord God, you fill your earth with people made in your image. And you call us to follow you and call us to serve each other in so many different ways. And two of these ways are through holy Matrimony and through Holy Orders. We ask you to, please, increase the number of those people who are called to those vocations and who say yes to those vocations. In Jesus' name we pray. Amen.

Dive **Deeper**

Are you single, married, or religious? Reflect upon your state in life. How can you live out the Gospel in your vocation? What are the joys and difficulties of your vocation?

Reflect on the **Faith**

- Marriage is an exchange between a man and a woman made to last as a faithful "partnership" for their entire lives, "ordered toward the good of the spouses and the procreation and education of offspring" (CCC 1601).

- The marriage covenant is an icon of the Trinity. Marriage also is made for the spouses' service of each other.

- Not all couples can have children naturally, which is a heavy cross for spouses to carry, but they are still able to engage in the marital act as husband and wife, which is naturally oriented toward procreation.

- The stable relationship between husband and wife provides the context for the education of offspring, that they can be raised in a stable environment.

- Scripture talks about marriage from the beginning to the end, from Adam and Eve—the marriage of the first man and first woman—to the Marriage Supper of the Lamb in the book of Revelation. Marriage is a critical image, especially the relationship of the Bridegroom, Jesus, to the Bride, the Church.

- "Marriage is not a purely human institution" because "God himself is the author of marriage," and we recognize that marriage predates every culture (CCC 1603).

- Marriage is the fundamental building block of society, where healthy families perpetuate healthy cultures and the breakdown of family leads to cultural breakdown.

Take It to **Prayer**

Father in heaven, in the name of your Son, Jesus Christ, we ask you to please receive our prayer this morning. Through the power of your Holy Spirit dwelling inside of us, that you give to us freely and give to us for our sanctification, for our salvation, for our growth, and becoming more and more like you, we ask you to please teach us today. We ask you to please help us to be docile to your movement, to your Word, to your vision for what marriage is supposed to be, what marriage is meant to be, and also how you can even work in our brokenness and you can still bring beauty out of ashes. So, Lord God, we ask you to please meet us in our need, especially those of us who have had difficult experiences when it comes to the sacrament of holy Matrimony—those who experience brokenness, those who experienced betrayal, those who have experienced hopes that have been crushed. We ask you to please be with all of us who have experienced that brokenness. And please be with those who are preparing for the great gift of Matrimony and those who are living in the great sacrament of Matrimony. Basically, Lord, be with all of us as we take these first steps in learning about your plan for marriage. In Jesus' name we pray. Amen.

Dive **Deeper**

Sacramental marriage is a complete gift of self. How does the Church view marriage as compared with the culture? Think of a happily married couple in your life that bears witness to the sacrament. What do they do to foster a mutual love?

Reflect on the **Faith**

- Even in the brokenness of our hearts and relationships since the Fall, the hope is that we will still learn how to love. But in our broken world after original sin, love always demands sacrifice.

- Even though marriage was always intended to be between one man and one woman, there are kings and other prominent figures who had multiple wives.

- God leads his people one step higher at a time so they are able to genuinely comprehend his teaching, starting with the dignity of the person and the importance of not possessing another human being as property.

- "Jesus unequivocally taught the original meaning of the union of man and woman," and when the Pharisees questioned him about Moses' allowing divorce, Jesus told them that it was only because of their "hardness of hearts" (CCC 1614). "But from the beginning it was not so" (Matthew 19:8).

- Jesus' teachings are not more of a load in their strictness than those of Moses. Instead, they help to renew the way man and woman were created to live, which sin distorted.

- Jesus "himself gives the strength and grace to live marriage in the new dimension of the Reign of God," giving us not just new rules but rather new hearts (CCC 1615).

- Grace changes our hearts, but we have to cooperate with that grace by carrying our crosses with Jesus.

Take It to **Prayer**

Father in heaven, we gather, we pray in the name of your Son, Jesus Christ. We pray in the power of your Holy Spirit that the gift you've given to us, the gift of life, the gift of love—because you are love, and you made us in your image and likeness—that these gifts, life and love, that we can embody them and live them out in our lives, in our relationships. Lord God, we know that you are everywhere. You are in healthy relationships, you are in broken relationships; you are in healthy people, you are in broken people. We know this because you are in our hearts, and we are both healthy and broken. We are both free and bound. The line of good and evil passes through our hearts, and you love our hearts. So help us, help us to see your plan for marriage in the Bible, to see your plan for marriage in Christ, to see your plan for marriage in our lives and in our world. We ask you this in the mighty name of Jesus Christ, our Lord. Amen.

Dive **Deeper**

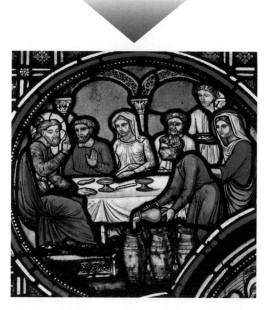

THE WEDDING FEAST AT CANA

Pictured here is the wedding feast at Cana, where Jesus miraculously changed water to wine. This miracle showed the importance of marriage, which Jesus made a sacrament (see CCC 1613).

Reflect on the **Faith**

- We recognize that Jesus said that there are those who give up marriage for the sake of the Kingdom. This does not mean that marriage is bad.

- St. John Chrysostom said, "Whoever denigrates marriage also diminishes the glory of virginity. Whoever praises it makes virginity more admirable and resplendent ...The most excellent good is something even better than what is admitted to be good" (quoted in CCC 1620).

- These consecrated virgins are living witnesses, in a hedonistic world, of joy and freedom without having a sexual relationship by giving themselves in love and service to the Lord.

- "The celebration of marriage ... normally takes place during Holy Mass," which is fitting because the Eucharist is the source and summit of all the Christian life (CCC 1621).

- The bride and groom "as ministers of Christ's grace mutually confer upon each other the sacrament of Matrimony by expressing their consent before the Church" (CCC 1623).

- There is something remarkable about the fact that once a couple is married, everything they do will be as a married couple. Their lives embody the sacrament. And the first thing that they will do together once married, during the wedding Mass, is pray.

- "The Holy Spirit is the seal of their covenant, the ever available source of their love and the strength to renew their fidelity" (CCC 1624).

Take It to **Prayer**

Father in heaven, O God, you're so good. You're so good that you give us these gifts, and we don't do anything to deserve them. You give us life, and we did nothing to deserve it. You give us love, and we did nothing to deserve it. You call us to be love in this world, to give love to the people around us, to be like you. And we don't even realize so often the great gifts that you continue to pour out on us. So Lord, please open our eyes so we can see your gifts. Open our hearts that we can be grateful for your gifts—the gift of life; the gift of the heart that is in our chest, the breath that is in our lungs; the ability to know who you are and to know that you have not forgotten us. And then even in our weakness and our woundedness, you've not abandoned us. Lord, help us to love well. Help us to be like you. And I make this prayer in the mighty name of Jesus Christ, our Lord. Amen.

Dive **Deeper**

Why are Catholics discouraged from having weddings outside of a church building (for example, outdoors)?

It is only natural for some couples to want their wedding to take place in a beautiful outdoor setting. The Church wants us to hold our weddings inside the sacred space of a church, though, because nature was marred by sin when Adam and Eve fell.

What the sacrament of Matrimony and consecrated places of worship have in common is that that they are the seeds of a renewed paradise. Christ came to restore and renew creation, to bring about a new heaven and a new earth, a place that will forever reflect God's glory as he intended. The traditional design and decorations of Catholic churches are meant to evoke and symbolize this new creation. The peace and beauty of a Catholic church, with Christ's Real Presence in the Eucharist at the heart, help show a couple that their married life is consecrated to God, set apart to carry him to a world in need of his saving presence.

Key reading: CCC 1042–1050, 1179–1186, 1607–1608, 1612

Reflect on the **Faith**

- For a couple to enter into marriage, they must have freedom, so there can be no impediments and they cannot be forced.

- Marriage is impossible between two people of the same sex.

- A couple must be able to enter into the sexual embrace in order for marriage to be a sacrament.

- Marriage is made real at the altar, in a public way, in the presence of the Church's minister and at least two witnesses. It is consummated and completed when the two become one flesh physically.

- Without consent to marry, "there is no marriage" (CCC 1626). There has to be a free act of the will.

- If the Church investigates a marriage and determines there was no impediment to marriage, it was a valid sacrament and the couple remains married even if they are civilly divorced.

- For those who believe that a case might be made that their marriage was null, talking to a priest for help is encouraged. The process for applying for a declaration of nullity is not meant to be burdensome. It is meant to be an opportunity for self-examination and a process of healing.

- Marriage is a sacrament of service and discipleship. A Catholic couple entering into the sacrament of Matrimony are saying that this is the way Jesus Christ is calling them to serve his Church and be his disciples, to build up the Body of Christ.

Take It to **Prayer**

Father in heaven, you are good. You are God. You are the Lord of life, and you're the Lord of love. We continue to praise your name. We continue to thank you for this gift of holy Matrimony. We thank you for the gift of faithfulness. We thank you for even the fact that when we were unfaithful, you remained faithful. Lord God, we thank you for mercy that comes to meet us in our weakness. We thank you for forgiveness that comes to us in our failures. And we thank you for never ceasing to call us to be more and more like you and for giving us the grace to be like you. We ask you to please help us to serve you, to love you, to honor you this day. And in whatever state in life we find ourselves, we give you our yes. And that yes is in Jesus' name. Amen.

Dive **Deeper**

Marriage is a covenant that mirrors the love of Christ and the soul. To dive deeper, watch the Ascension Presents YouTube video "Why Marriage Is NOT a Contract (It's a Covenant)."

Reflect on the **Faith**

- We believe that the fullness of truth subsists in the Catholic Church and that the fullness of discipleship, following after Jesus, subsists in the Catholic Church.

- Holy Matrimony is a sacrament of service, vocation, and discipleship— the way a couple plans to pursue the Lord, serve the Church, and build up the Kingdom of God.

- When a husband or wife is not pursuing the Lord with his or her whole heart, mind, soul, and strength, it can lead the other spouse to treat religion as unimportant.

- The whole point of getting married is to help your spouse become a saint and to help whatever children that come out of this marriage become saints.

- The Catholic person will almost always have to make the declaration that he or she intends to continue to live out the Faith in the Catholic Church.

- Both parties also need to declare that they will have their children baptized and raised and taught in the Catholic Faith.

- Wherever we find ourselves—unmarried, married to someone who shares the Faith, or married to someone who does not share the Faith—the call is always to say yes to God. Even in this broken world, every one of us is called to give God our yes in this moment and circumstance.

Take It to **Prayer**

Father in heaven, we give you glory, and we thank you for bringing us to this day. We thank you for the gift of life. We thank you for your teaching. We thank you for the vocations that you've called us to, various vocations, some that are named in these episodes and some that are not named in these episodes. We thank you for the variety that exists in your Church. And we ask you to please, wherever we find ourselves, whatever our state in life, whatever vocation we find ourselves in, help us to be faithful to that. Help us to not resent other people's vocations. Help us to be confident that wherever it is that we are, as long as we're saying yes to you, it is exactly where we should be, because it's exactly where we meet you. We make this prayer in the mighty name of Jesus Christ, our Lord. Amen.

Dive **Deeper**

Spend time praying for all married couples who struggle. Ask God to grant clarity to those seeking marriage and discerning their vocations.

Reflect on the **Faith**

- Marriage lasts until death and is between one husband and one wife.

- By entering into the sacrament of Matrimony, husbands and wives are strengthened by Jesus to carry their crosses with him.

- A husband and wife are called to offer each other forgiveness and love and to serve each other, motivated by love of Jesus. They receive the grace of the sacrament to do this.

- Jesus is the head of the Church, and he leads by laying down his life.

- Too many Christians have embraced the biblical idea that the father is the head of the household while forgetting the biblical idea of what it is to be the head. To be the head is to be the crucified one, the one who serves. We are not able to do that without the grace that comes from Jesus.

- The Head of the Church is active and serves. He lays down his life for his Bride, the Church. And the Church is in constant relationship with our Head, our Bridegroom.

- In marriage, the husband and wife have complementary roles, equal in dignity. They are both given the source of grace, Jesus Christ himself.

Take It to **Prayer**

Father in heaven, we give you thanks in the name of your Son, Jesus Christ. I'm praying in the power of the Holy Spirit. We ask that you please hear our prayer, receive our hearts, open our hearts, and heal our hearts. Lord God, there's so much in our lives that causes so much noise, so many things in our lives that can be helpful distractions and so many things in our lives that can be unhelpful or even destructive distractions. Lord God, we ask you to please clear out those destructive distractions, those things that take us away from what you want us to hear, those things that take us away from what it is that you want us to do. Lord God, we ask you to please take away from our hearts all things that could rob our hearts from love of you and love of our neighbor. Take away from our lives all those things that could steal our hearts from you and could cool our hearts from love of neighbor. Lord, I ask you on this day to please strengthen all of those couples that have been called to the sacrament of Matrimony. Please strengthen them in their love for each other. Strengthen them in their love for you. All those couples right now in this very moment that are struggling in their marriage, struggling in their vocation—we ask you to please give them the grace of patience. Give them the grace of mercy. Give them the grace of perseverance and give them the grace of hope. And remind them that their story is not over yet and that there are miles to go but they don't have to walk them alone. Lord God, be with this entire community in this moment. Open our hearts and fill them with your strength. In Jesus' name we pray. Amen.

Dive **Deeper**

Christ elevated marriage to the dignity of a sacrament. Reflect on the abundant graces received in marriage. How can even the struggles of marriage become opportunities of grace?

Reflect on the **Faith**

- The Church demands that we promise to love each other for life when we get married, which is also what love wants to do.

- Those who do not promise to love each other forever will find it very difficult to truly love one another for even one day.

- Marriage is about your spouse and no other until death, not about your spouse and no other until you get bored.

- In our broken world, in a regime of sin, circumstances such as violence can make it so that spouses cannot stay in the same home with each other. Then it is acceptable in the eyes of the Church for the husband and wife to move away from each other, but they remain a married couple.

- Each person is called to continually live out his or her vocation, so even if a husband and wife are no longer living in the same place, they are not free to pursue another relationship or marriage with someone else.

- Although it is very painful, those who are divorced and civilly remarried without a declaration from the Church that their previous marriage was null cannot receive Holy Communion. They cannot go to confession and receive absolution unless they have decided that they have repented and are resolved to live as brother and sister.

- When we understand the beauty and dignity of marriage, we know this is not an excessive command. But it is difficult.

Take It to **Prayer**

Father in heaven, we thank you. We give you praise. We give you glory. We honor you this day. And we ask that you please console us as we continue to learn more about what it is to have—what are the goods of married love? What are the requirements of married love? But don't just console us, Lord, because your Holy Spirit consoles, but your Holy Spirit also convicts. And so we ask you to please convict us as well. Convict us in truth and call us to be yours, not partially but fully. Because, Lord, you have covenanted yourself to us fully. And even when we are unfaithful, you are absolutely faithful. So be with us now. Console us and convict us, but above all, be with us. In Jesus' name we pray. Amen.

Dive **Deeper**

Reflect upon the tensions of marriage. What things can get in the way of a happy and holy married life? How can couples overcome these difficulties?

Reflect on the **Faith**

- Remember that the two ends of marriage are the good of the spouses (to get to heaven and be a saint) and the "procreation and education" of children (CCC 1652).

- The call of married life is the call to marriage and family, the call to be open to life.

- The sexual act is oriented, by its very nature, toward procreation, to fulfill the command in Scripture to "be fruitful and multiply" (CCC 1652; see Genesis 1:28).

- Marriage is not just about procreation but also about education, raising up children.

- The Church supports the many spouses who are open to life but have not been able to have children biologically.

- Those couples can still embrace a meaningful marriage that is filled with love, selflessness, and care for others.

- Another end of marriage is the good of the couple, helping each other be saints—and that is present also in times of grief and brokenheartedness.

- The home—the domestic church—is the first place where children learn the Faith and are taught forgiving, cheerful working, loving others as brothers and sisters, and especially worshipping God and praying.

- For those who are single and those who have no family of their own, the Church is there. It is not good for man to be alone. We need each other.

Take It to **Prayer**

Lord, you're good, and you've given us the gift of life. All life flows from you. All life, Lord God, flows from you. Your Holy Spirit—life exists where your Holy Spirit exists. Life radiates where your Holy Spirit penetrates. Lord God, we ask you to, please, penetrate our hearts with your Holy Spirit. Penetrate our relationships with your Holy Spirit so that your love, your life can radiate in our hearts, in our lives, in our relationships, especially those relationships, Lord, where it seems impossible, where it seems like there is no hope. Bring us that same Holy Spirit, that same Holy Spirit of hope, the same Holy Spirit of life, the same Holy Spirit of love, so that in this broken world, with our broken hearts, we can still be holy. We can still be yours. In Jesus' name we pray. Amen.

Dive **Deeper**

Reflect upon the gift of bringing children into the world. Take time to pray for couples with children and for couples who struggle to conceive.

Reflect on the **Faith**

- "The Christian home is the place where children receive the first proclamation of the faith. For this reason the family home is rightly called 'the domestic church'" (CCC 1666).

- We experience this world under the regime of sin, as those who suffer from the fall of Adam and Eve. And yet at the same time, Catholic families are meant to be domestic churches.

- We receive the sacraments not in a passive way but in an active way. When we sit down at Mass to hear the readings, being seated is not a posture of passivity but receptivity. It is like that with the sacraments: we have a posture of receptivity to God, who is initiating.

- The goal of our life is to be in union with Christ, God himself.

- Marriage is the fundamental building block of society, with husbands caring for their wives and wives caring for their husbands, forming a stable and lasting community from which comes life.

- It is essential that couples be open to life. Even if they cannot have biological children of their own, they still can have the kind of marriage that remains open to life, whether they pursue adoption or find a way to pour themselves out to the people around them.

- In the family we learn how to love.

Take It to **Prayer**

Father in heaven, we give you praise and glory. In the name of your Son, Jesus Christ, we ask that you please accept us. Receive us in the name of your Son, Jesus. By the power of your Holy Spirit, Lord God, help us to listen to your voice, especially in our brokenness—in this moment, Lord God, in our struggle, and especially if we're pressing play in a moment right now, Father, where we're just like, "I'm so far from you. I'm so far from you right now. I'm so far from living this life that you've called me to live. I'm so far from being faithful." But, God, meet us in this moment. Be with us in this moment. Meet us in our brokenness and help us to be unafraid to approach you. We have great fear of the Lord, yes, but let us not be afraid. And so we come before you, invoking the name of your Son, Jesus Christ, and claiming the promise of your Holy Spirit that helps us and enables us, gives us the power and the ability to pray. Be with us this day and every day. In Jesus' name we pray. Amen.

Dive **Deeper**

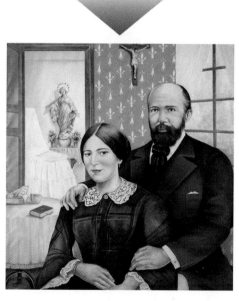

ST. LOUIS AND ST. ZÉLIE MARTIN

Pictured are Louis and Zélie Martin, the holy parents of St. Thérèse of Lisieux, who were canonized in 2015. They model for us Christ's love for the Church (see CCC 1661).

Reflect on the **Faith**

- Sacraments are sacred signs instituted by Christ that give grace. Sacramentals are also "sacred signs," put in place by the Church (CCC 1667). They prepare us to accept the grace that is given in the sacraments. They sanctify moments in our lives.

- An example of a sacramental is the use of holy water, reminding us of our Baptism and connecting us to our kingdom priesthood.

- When we bless something, we are setting it apart for a purpose. When something is blessed, it is made holy.

- Certain people also are consecrated, setting them apart for a particular ministry or mission in the Church.

- An exorcism takes place "when the Church asks publicly and authoritatively in the name of Jesus Christ that a person or object be protected against the power of the Evil One and withdrawn from his dominion" (CCC 1673).

- "A major exorcism" is done "only by a priest and with the permission of the bishop" (CCC 1673).

- We are called to use our kingdom priesthood by uniting our hearts with what is happening at the altar.

Take It to **Prayer**

Father in heaven, we give you praise and glory. We thank you. We thank you for the gifts that you have bestowed on us in your Church, not only the great gifts of your sacraments but the gifts of the sacramentals. The gifts not only that are just—are rooted in necessity, your Scripture, your Word, the Magisterium, your teaching, the Creed, and the sacraments but also these extra gifts, this "gravy," this "frosting," these "spices" that make life so good, that make following you—give it such vibrancy, these additional devotions that you give to us as means of reaching us in new ways and in different ways. Lord God, help us be open, especially if we're closed to the idea of devotionals or the idea of sacramentals. Help us to see them in their proper light. Help us to embrace the ones you're calling us to embrace and to honor and respect the ones that you're calling us to simply honor and respect. We make this prayer in the mighty name of Jesus Christ, our Lord. Amen.

Dive **Deeper**

There are many different sacramentals: holy water, rosaries, crucifixes, and many more. Do you have a favorite sacramental? How can it help foster your life of faith?

Reflect on the **Faith**

- In the moment in the baptismal rite when the Sign of the Cross is traced on the forehead of the person being baptized, the person is claimed for Christ.

- The Cross is a sign of suffering, sin, and brokenness, but it is transformed into being a sign of hope. We are marked by the death of Jesus in the sacraments, but Jesus embraced his Cross and conquered death and rose to life.

- Everything we do is oriented toward that last moment when we step from this life into eternal life. In the Nicene Creed, we say, "I look forward to the resurrection of the dead and the life of the world to come."

- The Christian meaning of death is revealed when we look at how Jesus died, a death marked by grief and struggle. Sweating blood in the Garden of Gethsemane, Jesus asked the Father to take the cup from him, but he embraced his Cross with trust in his Father.

- The homily during a funeral Mass should not be just a eulogy about the person. It should shed light on what death means for a Christian since Christ has risen from the dead. It invites the congregation to pray on behalf of the person who is in the casket.

- Most likely, the person whose funeral it is, even if he or she died in friendship with the Lord in a state of grace, will need the Mass to be offered up for the cleansing of the effects of his or her sins.

- It is easy to feel powerless in the face of death—but we are not powerless. As Catholics, we can still pray for the dead, offering Rosaries, the Chaplet of Divine Mercy, the Stations of the Cross, and Masses.

- Every time we go to Mass, we are participating in the great worship of heaven together with our loved ones who are in heaven. We always will see each other in the Eucharist.

Take It to **Prayer**

Father in heaven, we give you praise and glory and thank you. Thank you for bringing us to this day. Thank you for walking with us and leading us, by the guidance of your Church, through what we believe, through how we worship. Thank you for showing us the ways in which you want to be part of our lives. You want to transform our lives through your sacraments. And you do transform our lives through your sacraments. We come into contact with you, and you come into contact with us through your sacraments. Thank you for your Holy Spirit that makes actual what Jesus made possible. We thank you for this moment; we thank you for this opportunity today to learn about what every one of us will encounter in death. We ask you, please, help us to have minds and hearts that are open to participating in the funerals of those in our parishes, those in our families, those who are dear to us. And help us to understand the significance of life, the significance of death, the significance of eternal life, and how the funeral plays into all of that. We make this prayer in the mighty name of Jesus Christ, our Lord. Amen.

Dive **Deeper**

Death can be a difficult topic to think about, yet as Christians we have hope of eternal life. Although it might sound strange, take time to reflect on your own death. Are you ready? How can you prepare to meet God?

Reflect on the **Faith**

- Today Dr. Mary Healy joins us to introduce pillar three.

- In this third pillar of the *Catechism*, it comes down to our daily choices: Do I really believe what I say I believe?

- The first section of pillar three is about our vocation, life in the Holy Spirit. God never gives us a commandment that he does not empower us by the Holy Spirit to carry out.

- When we get to the challenging parts of the *Catechism*, we should take time to look Jesus in the eyes in prayer. In the gaze of Jesus, there is no room for pride or shame.

- We have a solemn obligation to form our conscience.

- Our bodies are who we are. How we live in the body determines our character, even for eternity. And so we have to treat the body with respect.

- Without freedom, we simply would not be human. We are given the incredible privilege of choosing the good.

- Three elements are absolutely crucial for living out this sometimes very challenging teaching: the mercy of God the Father, the truth of Jesus, and the power of the Holy Spirit.

- The Church's understanding of social justice is always founded on the dignity of the human person.

- Love, in its nature, is self-giving and about self-emptying and willing the other person's actual good, even though that may not be what the person thinks is good at the moment.

- Ultimately, the moral life is God calling us to the impossible. But what is impossible for men is possible for God. Every time we fall and then get up, it's a victory for the Kingdom.

- This part of the *Catechism* gets down to the concrete reality of our daily choices. Keep going. Be all in for Jesus because it is a complete adventure.

Take It to **Prayer**

Father in heaven, we give you praise and glory. Thank you for bringing us to the third pillar of the Catechism. Thank you for bringing us to this place where we can learn more about you, where we can know your identity and know our deepest identity as your beloved creation, as those who have been adopted by you in Baptism and made into your sons and your daughters. Help us to know you as our Father. Help us to know you, God, as Father, Son, and Holy Spirit and be drawn into your love. This day, we ask you to please bless this conversation. Bless Dr. Mary Healy, bless me, and please bless everyone who is listening to us today. In Jesus' name we pray. Amen.

Dive **Deeper**

Reflect on how often you consider what God has revealed about how he wants us to act. Do you make decisions with God or apart from him?

Reflect on the **Faith**

- We hear the Gospel proclaimed, are brought into communion with the Father, Son, and Holy Spirit through the sacraments, and are called to live new life as partakers of the divine nature and children of God.

- Our high call comes from God himself and from the dignity that he has given to us.

- Pope St. Leo the Great said, "Christian, recognize your dignity ... now that you share in God's own nature" (CCC 1691). Remember that, from Baptism, we are sons and daughters of God.

- We fall, but the Lord sustains us, giving us grace through the sacraments and prayer.

- Jesus has gone ahead of us, living in loving obedience to his Father, and we are called to follow in his footsteps toward heaven.

- There are many levels of catechesis.

- To be a saint, we have to acknowledge that we are sinners but also that God loves us and gives us mercy. Without acknowledging our sins, we would presume upon God's grace and presume that we would be going to heaven. Without God's mercy, we would be overwhelmed.

- Remember that we are God's, and "he longs for you to use all that is in you, as if it were his own, for the service and glory of the Father" (CCC 1698).

Take It to **Prayer**

Father in heaven, we give you thanks and praise. We thank you for yesterday. Thank you for Dr. Mary Healy. Thank you for not only, just, like we talked about when it came to marriage, the invitation and the challenge—when it comes to the Christian life, the invitation and the challenge, the blessing and the burden, the rights we have as sons and daughters of God and the responsibilities we have as sons and daughters of God. God, thank you. Thank you. But also, please help us. Help us as we take these next steps to recognize our dignity, to recognize the high call, and to recognize your mercy when we fail, to recognize the ways in which we do need to be shaped, that our consciences do need to be formed, that we do need to be trained in this catechesis. Help us to be open to your Holy Spirit. Help us to be open to this high call. Help us to be open to both the conviction of sin and the conviction of mercy. In Jesus' name we pray. Amen.

Dive **Deeper**

Reflect on the theological and moral teachings of the Church that are easiest to accept. Which teachings of the Church are most difficult for you to accept? How can you continue to grow in this area?

Reflect on the **Faith**

- Because we have been redeemed and God has poured out his Holy Spirit into us, we have to live in a certain way.

- Article 1 tells us that Jesus reveals us entirely to ourselves—who and what we are, where we come from, where we are going, and why we are.

- "In a plan of sheer goodness," God wants us to "share in his own blessed life" (CCC 1). We are made in God's "image and likeness" (CCC 1701).

- From the very beginning of our existence, from the very moment of our conception, human beings are destined for eternal beatitude, for heaven.

- We believe we have a destination we are made for. God made every person for heaven. Even if a person does not choose heaven, that is what God made us all for—to be united with him for eternity.

- Since we are made in God's image and likeness, we have an intellect, so we can understand the order of things in the world. We also have free will, which we use to choose the good and the beautiful and the truth.

- Though humanity fell through original sin and human beings do evil, in our nature we are still good and want the good.

- Jesus came to set us free from the Devil and sin so we could live. He earned that for us, and "his grace restores what sin had damaged in us" (CCC 1708).

Take It to **Prayer**

Father in heaven, we give you praise. Thank you so much. Thank you for this group of people. Thank you for this community of CIYers. Thank you for helping each one of us today to press play. Thank you for helping each one of us today to be open, once again, to your high call, to be open, once again, to what it is—not just what you want from us but what you want for us. You've made us in your very image. And you call us to treat everyone we meet as they are made, in your image. So today, Father, we don't just want to have the idea that every human person has dignity, we want to have the reality, we want to have that change our actions: how we look at people, how we treat people, how we speak to them, how we think of them. Help us to never, ever forget that the people surrounding us are made in your image and likeness. The people surrounding us have an incredible dignity that cannot be taken away. Help us to treat each other in that dignity and to treat ourselves with that dignity. And by doing so, help us to honor you. In Jesus' name we pray. Amen.

Dive **Deeper**

Choose one of the four cardinal virtues to foster this week—justice, fortitude, temperance, or prudence. Ask God for assistance in building a life of virtue.

Reflect on the **Faith**

- "Beatitude" can be translated as "blessing" and "happiness," the ultimate good to which God has called us. The beatific vision is that happiness, the blessed vision of heaven. God has made us for himself, and God alone satisfies.

- The Beatitudes from the Sermon on the Mount fulfill in the Kingdom of heaven God's promises to Abraham: worldwide blessing, a dynasty, and land.

- True happiness is not the fleeting happiness of mere pleasure.

- We want to know not just the words in the Bible, but God. For, as St. Thomas Aquinas said, "God alone satisfies" (CCC 1718).

- As the *Baltimore Catechism* said, "God made me to know Him, to love Him, and to serve Him in this world, and to be happy with Him for ever in heaven." (See CCC 1721.)

- We get to choose between good and evil, life and death. "True happiness is … in God alone" (CCC 1723).

- Where we spend our time and our money is where we place our hearts.

- We have many moral choices and need to ask, "What gets my heart above everything else? Is it going to be the Lord—or anything else?"

Take It to **Prayer**

*Father in heaven, we ask you to please send us an abundance of your
Holy Spirit so that we can truly love you with our whole heart, mind, soul,
and strength, that we can love you with everything. Lord God, the world presents
to us so many alternatives to goodness, so many alternatives to truth, so many
alternatives to true beauty. We ask you to please help us to choose you. Help us
choose the truth. Help us to choose beauty. Help us to choose goodness. So help
us to choose you. God, you will never abandon us. Help us to never abandon you.
In Jesus' name we pray. Amen.*

Dive **Deeper**

THE SERMON ON THE MOUNT

It was during his Sermon on the Mount that Jesus taught the Beatitudes (see CCC 1716).

Reflect on the **Faith**

- We have been given an intellect, so we can know the good, the true, and the beautiful. Because we are rational beings with wills, we have the power and capacity to choose. We have freedom.

- Freedom is not simply the ability to do whatever we want, but freedom is the power to do what is right, the power to do what we ought.

- Who we choose to be earlier in life is who we ultimately end up becoming later in life.

- There is sin on earth because we have the capacity to say either yes or no to God. In heaven, our freedom has been perfected.

- To sin is not to become free but to become a slave.

- In heaven there is no sin, but we are completely free to be constantly choosing God, to love each other and the Lord as we are supposed to.

- Because we have freedom, we have responsibility.

- Certain factors can reduce responsibility and culpability.

- If we are going to exercise our freedom, we also have to be willing to take responsibility.

Take It to **Prayer**

Father in heaven, we give you thanks and praise and thank you, again. And thank you so much for your goodness. Thank you so much for bringing us to this day, for bringing us to this moment. Thank you for giving us an intellect to think. Thank you for giving us a will that we can choose. Thank you for creating us in your image and likeness and conferring on us this dignity and this power. Thank you for the power to do good. Thank you for the power to choose the good. Help us to always, always turn away from evil. Help us to always, always turn toward you and, in turning towards you, experience that beatitude, experience that blessing, experience that fullness that is you and that fullness that comes from choosing you. Give us this power because, Lord, we often find ourselves too weak to choose. Give us the power to do the right. In Jesus' name we pray. Amen.

Dive **Deeper**

Freedom is not the ability to do what we want to do but what we ought to do. How does this change your perception of freedom? Does our culture value true freedom or a false sense of freedom?

Reflect on the **Faith**

- Due to the Fall, there was a darkening of the intellect, so we can know, but we do not always know fully or clearly. There was also a weakening of the will, so we can choose, but we do not always choose with strength.

- We can use our freedom for the wrong thing.

- We have "freely sinned." As often as we have chosen sin, we "became a slave to sin," doing to ourselves what Adam and Eve did to the human race (CCC 1739).

- By our nature, we are still good and still retain God's image, yet that image has been marred and broken. Our freedom has become wounded.

- Our culture needs to be reminded that "the exercise of freedom does not imply a right to say or do everything"; true freedom is the power to do what I ought to do, to choose the good and the truth (CCC 1740).

- The moral law is not a straitjacket as much as it is a set of good guideposts that give us the ability to live with freedom and joy.

- The grace that God gives us does not overwhelm our free will. We know that we cannot choose and do good without God's help. Jesus is the vine and we are the branches. Apart from him, we can do nothing. (See John 15:5.)

- We need God's grace and the power that comes from him. This corresponds with our freedom, giving us the capacity to do what we ought to do.

Take It to **Prayer**

Father in heaven, you are good, and you are God. You are Lord. You're the author of life, and you are the one who gave us freedom. You're the one who made us in your image and likeness so that we could live freely, so that we could use our freedom to love, so that we could use our freedom to be like you. We ask you this day, help us. Help us by your grace. Help us by your constant assistance to choose you, to cling to you, and to live as you. Jesus Christ, you are the Lord of life. Send us your Holy Spirit that we can walk with you as our Lord this day and every day. In Jesus' name we pray. Amen.

Dive **Deeper**

ST. PAUL IN PRISON BY REMBRANDT

This painting by Rembrandt shows St. Paul held in prison. The real threat to human freedom is not physical chains but sin, and thus in Christ St. Paul is free indeed (see CCC 1740).

Reflect on the **Faith**

- Because we have freedom, we have agency, which means that we can choose.

- Because we can choose between right and wrong, because we have freedom, we make moral choices. Each of us is a moral subject.

- So often in the world's view, things are only right or wrong if you have the opinion that they are right or wrong or that they do or do not work. Actions are often evaluated based on either preference or utility, not actual, objective right or wrong.

- Yet we recognize that "the morality of human acts depends on" three objective elements: "the object chosen" (the thing itself), "the end in view or the intention" (why I did it), and "the circumstances of the action" (CCC 1750).

- For a human act to be fully "*morally good*," all three of those must be morally good.

- For example, for a book to be good, it needs good writing, well-developed characters, and a good plot. If one of those is missing, it falls short and is not good.

- "The end does not justify the means" (CCC 1753).

- "One may not do evil so that good may result from it" (CCC 1756).

- A bad intention or a bad circumstance can make the whole moral act evil. And if the object chosen is evil, the best of intentions and the best of circumstances cannot make that a good action.

Take It to **Prayer**

Father in heaven, we give you praise and thank you so much. Thank you for making us like you. Thank you for giving us an intellect and a will. Thank you for calling us to love, making us in your image so that we can—so we can love. We are sorry for the times we have failed to love. Help us. Help us in our weakness. We are truly sorry for all the times that we have not risen above our brokenness, for all the times we've not said yes to your grace, for all the times we've done the wrong thing in the right way or for the wrong reason or the right thing for the wrong way or wrong reason. For all the ways, Lord, we just have violated your law, violated your will, and broken your heart, we are sorry. We ask you to help us. Receive our broken hearts. Receive our wounded hearts. And help us to belong to you this day and every day. In Jesus' name we pray. Amen.

Dive **Deeper**

In moral theology, the intention is part of what makes an action good. Ask God to help you purify your intentions today.

Reflect on the **Faith**

- The will is what enables us to choose. The appetite is what draws us and moves us.

- "In themselves passions are neither good nor evil" (CCC 1767). At the same time, what we do with them is where we either grow in virtue or grow in vice. We can feed our passions and channel them. They are drivers that move us to do things.

- "The most fundamental passion is love, aroused by the attraction of the good" (CCC 1765). "To love is to will the good of the other" (CCC 1766).

- The other inclinations are based on the inclination "toward the good," for "only the good can be loved" (CCC 1766).

- Just because someone has an enthusiastic or deep conviction and is passionate about something, that doesn't make that thing good or make that person virtuous. Anytime it is not for the good, it is something other than love.

- "Passions are morally good when they contribute to a good action" but morally evil when they contribute to an evil action (CCC 1768).

- The Holy Spirit is the one who helps us bring the passions, intellect, and will together to form a person who is holy.

- Freedom is found when not only our intellect apprehends the true and our will is choosing the good, but also when our desires and passions are oriented toward the good and we want to actually do the right thing.

- The goal is not to eliminate our desires but to reorient and transform them.

Take It to **Prayer**

Father in heaven, we give you thanks. Truly, truly, you have given us—you've made us human beings with bodies and souls. Those bodies—we have desires in our hearts. We have desires in our bodies. We have desires in ourselves, in our psyche, Lord God, and you've made us. You've given us these, so many of these desires. But also, so many of these desires have become distorted. So many of these desires have experienced the result of the Fall. We experience fear where we should not fear. We experience bravado where we should be humble. We experience greed where we have enough. We experience all of these emotions—anger when we're not justified in this. Or, Lord God, we know that sometimes our justified emotions we act on in not good ways. We twist them. We feed those that shouldn't be fed, and we don't feed those that should be fed. Lord God, just give us clarity today. In the midst of our passions, in the midst of this call to live a moral life and a good life, we ask that you please refine our emotions, refine our passions. Make those that should be strong, strong. And make those that should be said no to, give us the ability to have a will that is in charge of our passions. Give us the ability to have an intellect that knows when it's the right thing to run and when it's the right thing to stand and fight. Lord God, help, give us an intellect that knows when to act and when not to act. And give us strong passions—strong passions so that we can respond to life with power and with strength. In Jesus' name we pray. Amen.

Dive **Deeper**

Often our passions can incline us to do things that lead to sin. Examine the places in your life where you feel like your passions are leading you. This can be with food, shopping, your cell phone, or any number of things. Make a small sacrifice and give up that thing that your passions are leading you to grasp for a period.

Reflect on the **Faith**

- Human beings have a conscience within themselves. *Gaudium et Spes* tells us that it reveals a "law" that a person "has not laid upon himself but which he must obey ... ever calling him to love and to do what is good and to avoid evil" (CCC 1776).

- Just because we have a sense that something is right or wrong does not make it so. Our conscience can be malformed, numbed, or deafened. God wants us to have a well-formed conscience.

- The world often sees conscience as our gut feeling, but it is actually "a judgment of reason" (CCC 1778). The work of our intellect is necessary, and it has the ability to apprehend truth.

- The louder the voice of the world around us becomes, the harder it becomes to hear the voice of conscience. Each of us must be "present to himself"; we must remove the distractions (CCC 1779).

- We need to understand the "principles of morality" and "their application," practically choosing between goods and competing goods (CCC 1780).

- When we have freedom, we have responsibility. Conscience lets us be responsible for what we do.

- When we reach out to do what is evil, the voice of conscience in us tells us it was wrong and reminds us of what is good.

- Conscience reminds us that we need to seek to be forgiven and that there are good things to be chosen.

Take It to **Prayer**

Father in heaven, we give you praise. We give you glory. We thank you. We ask you to, please, receive us. Lord, we are here to learn. We are here as disciples. We are not here to tell you how you should be. We're not here to tell you how you should look at us, how you should treat us, how you should make us. We're not here to tell you anything. We're just simply here to learn. We're here to be formed by you. We're here to be taught by you. We're here to be changed and transformed by you. So, Lord God, we ask—we bring before you our conscience, our conscience that has been in some ways malformed, our conscience that's been wounded, our conscience that's been deafened, our conscience that's been hardened and in rebellion, and so often ways we need to be softened, and we need to be taught. Lord God, transform our conscience; transform our inner world. Transform our hearts so we can be more and more like you this day and every day. In Jesus' name we pray. Amen.

Dive **Deeper**

To become virtuous we need "a well-formed conscience" (CCC 1783). Take time today to examine the things that form you. Do you allow Jesus and the wisdom of the Church to form you, or do you allow the internet, work, and social circles to form you instead?

Reflect on the **Faith**

- No one can force us to do something, and yet our conscience has to be formed. Educating our conscience is work that continues throughout our lifetimes.

- We use our reason to form our conscience well. We need to have good reasons for what we believe.

- We also are born with broken hearts and dimmed intellects, so the formation of conscience is very important because sin pulls us toward wanting to follow our own way.

- We are to learn what the good is, what God's Law tells us about the right way to live, but then we have to actually choose it in our day-to-day life. It is not just an information transfer, but a transformation.

- Our conscience needs to be looked at in light of what love looks like: the kind of love shown by Jesus on the Cross.

- It is always true that, even in a complex world, a person must "never do evil so that good may result from it" (CCC 1789).

- The Golden Rule always holds true: do to others what you would have them do to you.

- We always must show care for others and their conscience, and we must never cause our brothers and sisters to fall.

Take It to **Prayer**

Father in heaven, we give you praise, and we call upon your name. We call upon the name of your Son, Jesus Christ. We ask for your Holy Spirit to be sent upon us this day that we can truly know the good and our minds be formed—our intellects, our reason be formed to the truth, but also that our will is conformed to the good, that also we have the strength to do the good, not simply know the good but to choose the good. And so we ask you, please, Lord God, console our conscience where we need to be consoled. Convict our conscience where we need to be convicted, and help us to become the kind of people that can live in this world, this complicated and complex world, like saints. In your name, we pray. Amen.

Dive **Deeper**

Often it feels easier to lie about small things than to tell the truth. If this is something you struggle with, make a resolution to tell the truth even in difficult moments this week. Ask God for grace to help you.

Reflect on the **Faith**

- Someone who purposely does what his conscience tells him is wrong "would condemn himself" (CCC 1790)

- "Certain judgment" is when we know that something is true, good, wrong, or evil. We have to follow conscience's "certain judgment," but our conscience can make mistakes (CCC 1790). We must take every opportunity to know what is right.

- Sin can also deaden our conscience. God is the one who helps us see and hear.

- We are rational beings made in God's image and likeness, and it is our job to find out what the true, the good, and the beautiful is. If we choose against those things, choosing the ugly and the evil, and we become blinded by sin, then it is our fault.

- There are times where our "ignorance is invincible"—that means there was no way we could have or should have known something (CCC 1793). Our responsibility and culpability for erroneous judgment is mitigated, maybe even eradicated.

- Even if we did not know, an evil action is still evil, and we must continue in the process of forming our conscience.

- All of us are called to become virtuous because we are called to be free.

- Having a formed conscience is an invitation to be free, strong, courageous, and powerful in this world.

- Remember that freedom is the power to do what we ought. If we had this power, we would have joy.

- We "must always obey the certain judgment of … conscience," and yet that conscience must be well formed (CCC 1790).

Take It to **Prayer**

Father in heaven, we give you praise. We give you glory. We ask you to, please, open our minds so that we can truly apprehend the truth, we can truly apprehend the good, the beautiful. And give us hearts and wills that are strong and courageous, that can actually choose what we know is true and refuse to do what we know is evil. Help us always to turn away from evil, even in small ways, Lord God. There are some things that are obviously evil, some things that are— that we would say are beyond the pale, we would never choose those. Lord, we ask you to, please, help us to choose against those when they're small. Help us to choose against those when they're little. Help us to choose against those when we just tolerate evil in our lives. Help us to not tolerate evil in our lives. The evil that we not only tolerate but sometimes we delight in—help us to never do that. Help us to delight in you. Help us to delight in virtue. Help us to delight in truth and goodness and beauty. In Jesus' name we pray. Amen.

Dive **Deeper**

Examine your life and consider any habitual sins that blind your conscience. Create a plan to root out those things slowly but effectively. This will take patience and grace, but do not be afraid to start your journey.

Reflect on the **Faith**

- The cardinal virtues are the hinge virtues—prudence, justice, temperance, and fortitude—which are necessary for a healthy and free life.

- The moral life is a life of freedom. To embrace responsibility and choose to live according to the Commandments is to ultimately live a life of freedom and of happiness.

- The virtues are not straitjackets. They are "firm attitudes, stable dispositions, habitual perfections of intellect and will that govern our actions, order our passions, and guide our conduct according to reason and faith" (CCC 1804).

- A virtue is not about *occasionally* doing what is good. What makes a person virtuous is not sometimes telling the truth or being prudent or temperate. Instead "a virtue is an habitual and firm disposition to do the good" (CCC 1803).

- A person who has virtue does what is good without being forced to do it. But it takes human effort. We have to discipline ourselves, bear fruit in trial, and embrace God's grace.

- The first cardinal virtue is prudence. Prudence is doing the right thing at the right time in the right way.

- Justice involves giving another being—family, our country, God—what we owe them. And we owe God everything.

- Fortitude provides for all the other virtues at the moments of testing, when they are needed most. With it, we can actually lay down our lives for what is right.

- Temperance is using good things at the right time in the right way.

Take It to **Prayer**

Father in heaven, we give you praise. We give you glory. We ask for an outpouring of your Holy Spirit upon our lives, into our hearts in this moment. We ask you to give us the grace to live a life of virtue. We ask you to give us the grace to live a life of freedom and of joy, to do the right even when it's difficult, to choose the good thing even when it's hard to choose, and in that to be conformed in such a way to your will and to your grace that we choose it with ease. So we pray all this in the mighty name of Jesus Christ, our Lord. Amen.

Dive **Deeper**

Reflect upon the four cardinal virtues: justice, temperance, fortitude, and prudence. Which of these is easiest for you to practice? Which of these do you struggle with?

Reflect on the **Faith**

- The theological virtues of faith, hope, and love are necessary to live the Christian life. God is the source and the "why" of these virtues. These virtues direct us to him.

- In order to have theological virtues, we need grace. "Human virtues," which we gain by being taught and by practice, are raised up through the gift of God's grace (CCC 1810).

- To be a free and flourishing human being, we need the human, cardinal virtues—prudence, temperance, justice, and fortitude—but "to live in a relationship with the Holy Trinity," we also need the virtues of faith, hope, and love (CCC 1812). These virtues come from God himself.

- We have faith in God. We hope in God, regardless of where life leads us. We love him.

- Unless we have faith, there is always going to be a skeptic that lives inside us. But when we have encountered the living God and we hear what he reveals, our questions come not from cynicism or skepticism but from wanting to understand.

- Theology is faith seeking understanding. We don't ask God to "prove it" before we will have faith. We have faith because we trust God.

- Faith requires action. We are saved by grace—God's free gift— through faith working itself out in love.

- With the gift of faith, we become missionaries, for in addition to accepting the Faith, we declare the Faith.

Take It to **Prayer**

Father in heaven, we give you glory; we give you praise. We thank you for bringing us here. I thank you, God, for every person who's been journeying these 242 days through the Catechism, desiring to know you and your will better, to know how to worship you, to know who you are in yourself and who you are with us. We ask you, continue to help us know how you are calling us to live. And, God, as we learn about the theological virtues, particularly faith, we ask that you please meet us with your grace to give us that gift of faith and help us to live out the virtue of faith. We make this prayer in the mighty name of Jesus Christ, our Lord. Amen.

Dive **Deeper**

Reflect upon the three theological virtues: faith, hope, and love. These are at the heart of our lives as Catholics. Which is easiest for you to practice, and which is hardest?

Reflect on the **Faith**

- For many of us, hope refers to a wish and a kind of optimism. But hope is more than that, for it is linked to "desire" (CCC 1817).

- Stoicism—a dispassionate approach to life with the sense that this is how life is and I am going to accept it—is not complete and not Christianity. One reason is that we are called to have hope, whereby we desire something.

- What we desire are the right things: "the kingdom of heaven and eternal life as our happiness" (CCC 1817). We are called to stir up this desire and should be asking God for it.

- With hope, we also "trust in Christ's promises ... relying not on our own strength" (CCC 1817).

- Hope is trust in another, extended into the future. We surrender our whole selves to God because we trust that he is here, that he is good, and that he loves us.

- We do not have confidence based on ourselves but on the Holy Spirit's aid.

- God has given to every single one of us this desire to be happy. Hope "purifies" our desire to be known and to have a life worth living—not for the world, but for God (CCC 1818).

- Hope helps us not to be discouraged, uplifting us when we feel alone. Hope enables us to be selfless.

- We are called to hope that the grace of God will preserve us to the end.

Take It to **Prayer**

Father in heaven, we give you praise. We do. We love you. And we thank you. We glorify your name in this moment and every moment. We ask that you please send upon us in the name of your Son, Jesus Christ, by the power of your Holy Spirit, the grace of hope. Give us the grace of faith and love. But give us the grace of hope today that we can trust in your promises. By faith, we trust in your presence. And by hope, we trust in your promises. And we just ask you, please, seal that gift and strengthen that virtue so that we can be yours this day and every day. We make this prayer in the mighty name of Jesus Christ, our Lord. Amen.

Dive **Deeper**

Hope is the virtue that compels us to live with heaven in mind. Watch the Ascension Presents YouTube video about the virtue of hope called "What Is Hope and Why Do You Need It?"

Reflect on the **Faith**

- Charity is a particular kind of love.

- Jesus tells us that the greatest of the Commandments is love. Love is the fulfillment of the Commandments.

- One of the ways we know we are loving God is if we are loving our neighbor. "This is my commandment, that you love one another as I have loved you" (John 15:12, quoted in CCC 1823).

- Jesus also makes a very clear connection between obeying the Commandments of God and loving God.

- If we want to have a personal relationship with God, we must strive to obey what he has said in the Commandments; it is not optional.

- Love is not just in the heart but must be translated into action. The virtue of charity has to be *effective*, not just *affective*. An effective love is love that moves and acts.

- When we are filled by love, trying to turn away from evil and live a moral life makes us free. We do not approach God like a slave or like someone who just wants payment.

- St. Basil says that "if we obey for the sake of the good itself and out of love for him who commands ... we are in the position of children" (CCC 1828).

- It is clear that in the practice of the moral life we have to do what God asks by following his Commandments. But all of this is to be brought alive through charity and a relationship with the Father in order to have "the spiritual freedom of the children of God" (CCC 1828).

Take It to **Prayer**

Father in heaven, we know that you are love. We know that you are the fullness of everything that we desire. We know that you're the source of all love and that none of us can actually love without you because you are love. In this moment, Lord God, we ask you to send your Holy Spirit of charity, your Holy Spirit of love into our hearts, that we can love you above all things and we can love our neighbor as ourselves. And that even though we have the ability, the power, the virtue to be able to love ourselves—because, Lord God, until we love you, until we love ourselves, we can never love our neighbor, we definitely can't love our enemy. And so, God, help us. Help us to love you. Help us to love ourselves. Help us to love our friends and family, our neighbors. And even, Lord, help us to love our enemies. Help us to love those who have hurt us. Give us this power now and always. We pray in the name of the Father, and of the Son, and of the Holy Spirit. Amen.

Dive **Deeper**

Love is the most important virtue. How can you love more freely, as Christ does? Who is God asking you to love most especially today?

CONCLUDING SUMMARY

The second part of the *Catechism* proclaims and explains how God in his great goodness communicates his life to us today in ways that beautifully fit and elevate our nature. He does this so that we can respond to his invitation of love to share in his eternal happiness by uniting ourselves freely to him in the liturgy and the sacraments. The heart of his goodness is expressed and made real in the Eucharist, in which we can come to share in the divinity of Christ, who first came to share in our humanity.

CONCLUDING QUESTIONS AND ANSWERS

1. **What are the seven sacraments?**

   Baptism, Confirmation, Holy Eucharist, Reconciliation (or Penance), Anointing of the Sick, Holy Orders, and Matrimony.

2. **Did Christ institute each of the sacraments?**

   Yes (see CCC 1114).

3. **What does the phrase "*lex orandi, lex credendi*" mean?**

   It means "the law of prayer is the law of faith: the Church believes as she prays" (CCC 1124).

4. **Why are the sacraments efficacious?**

   Because it is Christ who works in each of them (see CCC 1127).

5. **What does it mean to say that the sacraments act "*ex opere operato*"?**

   It means "'by the very fact of the action's being performed' ... i.e., by virtue of the saving work of Christ, accomplished once for all" (CCC 1128).

6. **In Baptism, what does the white garment symbolize?**

   It symbolizes that the person has now "put on Christ" (CCC 1243).

7. **In Confirmation, who is the minister of the sacrament?**

   In both Eastern and Western rites, it is the bishop, although he may delegate this faculty to a priest (see CCC 1312–1314).

8. **What are the two great "parts" that make up the Mass?**

They are the liturgy of the Word and the liturgy of the Eucharist (see CCC 1346).

9. **What are some of the other names we can give to the Eucharist?**

The Holy Eucharist can also be called the Lord's Supper, the Breaking of Bread, the Eucharistic assembly, the memorial of the Lord's passion and resurrection, the Holy Sacrifice, the Holy and Divine Liturgy, the Sacred Mysteries, the Most Blessed Sacrament, Holy Communion, and Holy Mass (see CCC 1328–1332).

10. **What is an indulgence?**

"An indulgence is a remission before God of the temporal punishment due to sins whose guilt has already been forgiven" (CCC 1471).

11. **What are the two main effects of the sacrament of Penance and Reconciliation?**

Reconciliation with God and reconciliation with his Church (CCC 1468–1469).

12. **Can a person receive the sacrament of the Anointing of the Sick more than once?**

Yes (see CCC 1514–1515).

13. **What is "Viaticum"?**

It is the sacrament of the Eucharist offered to those who are about to die (see CCC 1524–1525).

14. **What is the overall title given in the *Catechism* to the two sacraments of Holy Orders and Matrimony?**

Sacraments at the service of communion (see CCC 1211 and 1533).

15. **Which three of the sacraments confer an "indelible spiritual character" and so cannot be repeated?**

    Baptism, Confirmation, and Holy Orders (see CCC 1582).

16. **In the Latin Church, who are understood to be the ministers of Christ's grace in the sacrament of Matrimony?**

    The spouses themselves (see CCC 1623).

17. **What is the "indispensable element" of marriage?**

    The free consent of the couple (see CCC 1625–1628).

18. **What is the main feast in the liturgical year?**

    Easter (see CCC 1168–1169).

19. **What is the Liturgy of the Hours?**

    The daily public prayer of the Church (1174–1178).

20. **What is another name for the "ambo"?**

    The lectern (see CCC 1184).

NOTES

1. "About 24% of Catholics in the United States attended Mass every week or more often prior to the COVID-19 pandemic in 2019. In … late summer 2022, 17% of adult Catholics reported attending Mass this frequently." In "Where is Mass Attendance Highest and Lowest?" *1964* (blog), Center for Applied Research in the Apostolate (CARA), January 23, 2023, nineteensixty-four.blogspot.com.

2. Quoted in Christopher West, "John Paul II's Theology of the Body: Key to an Authentic Marital and Family Spirituality," Crossroads Initiative, February 9, 2016, crossroadsinitiative.com.

3. International Theological Commission, "The Hope of Salvation for Infants Who Die Without Being Baptised," (2007), vatican.va.

4. Paul VI, *Paenitemini* (February 17, 1966), chap. 1, vatican.va.

ILLUSTRATION CREDITS

Day 121: "Ascension of Christ," jorisvo/stock.adobe.com.

Day 128: Albrecht Dürer, *Adoration of the Trinity*—Landauer Altarpiece (1511), in Kunsthistorisches Museum, Vienna, Adam Ján Figeľ/stock.adobe.com.

Day 133: Diego Velazquez, *The Coronation of the Virgin* (1635–1636), Shalone/stock.adobe.com.

Day 135: "The fresco of Resurrection in church kostel Svateho Cyrila Metodeje probably by František Sequens," Renáta Sedmáková/stock.adobe.com.

Day 139: "Vision of Angels–Dante," Archivist/stock.adobe.com.

Day 141: Michelangelo, *The Last Judgment* (1537–1541), in the Sistine Chapel, Rome, Agcreativelab/stock.adobe.com.

Day 148: "Espíritu Santo," JorgeAlberto/stock.adobe.com.

Day 152: "Catholic mass. Open Roman missal on altar" (2018), France, Godong/stock.adobe.com.

Day 156: "Altar with chalice and Missal during a traditional old latin rite Mass," t0m15/stock.adobe.com.

Day 157: "Vintage book for music in the Catholic church," tsezarina/stock.adobe.com.

Day 160: "Latin liturgical calendar for years 532–626 AD on marble," Ravenna, shapencolour/alamy.com.

Day 162: Giovanni Francesco Barbieri, *Christ and the Woman of Samaria at the Well* (1640–1641), in the Thyssen-Bornemisza Museum, Madrid, Godong Photo/stock.adobe.com.

Day 167: Svjatoslav Hordynskyj, *Baptism of Christ* (1983–1985), in Barbarakirche church, Renáta Sedmáková/stock.adobe.com.

Day 170: "Baptism ceremony in Church," Надія Коваль/stock.adobe.com.

Day 172: "Jesus teaches Nicodemus … ," fluenta/stock.adobe.com.

Day 175: August Müller, *Pentecost* (1923), in the church Dreifaltigkeitskirche, Bern, jozef sedmak/stock.adobe.com.

Day 177: "Confirmation sponsor," AG Photo Design/stock.adobe.com.

Day 180: Juan de Juanes, *The Last Supper* (1560s), corvalola/stock.adobe.com.

Day 181: Michele Rapisardi, *The Supper at Emmaus* (1858), Renáta Sedmáková/stock.adobe.com.

Day 183: "Golden Chalices on the Altar with Priest," peacepix/stock.adobe.com.

Day 185: "Icon of Cain and Abel offering their sacrifices to God," in the church of the Exaltation of the Venerable Cross, Bratislava, Adam Ján Figeľ/stock.adobe.com.

Day 187: "Eucharistic adoration of angels" (1932), in Chiesa di Santa Maria Assunta E. Lancia, Morgex, Renáta Sedmáková/stock.adobe.com.

Day 188: "Hands of a priest consecrating a host as the body of Christ to distribute it to the communicants in the church" (2023), Davizro Photography/stock.adobe.com.

Day 193: Hubert and Jan van Eyck, *The Adoration of the Mystic Lamb* (1432), in Saint Bavo Cathedral, Ghent, Pecold/stock.adobe.com.

Day 199: "Priest in confession booth," Anneke/stock.adobe.com.

Day 202: Pompeo Girolamo Batoni, *The Return of the Prodigal Son* (1773), in Kunsthistorisches Museum, Vienna, Adam Ján Figeľ/stock.adobe.com.

Day 203: "Souls in purgatory," zatletic/stock.adobe.com.

Day 208: "Trnava – The neo-gothic fresco the Apostles at viaticum," Renáta Sedmáková/stock.adobe.com.

Day 217: de Ferrari, *Christ Washing the Disciples' Feet* (1520–1525), Renáta Sedmáková/stock.adobe.com.

Day 220: "Wedding at Cana," stained glass window from Saint Germain-l'Auxerrois church in Paris, France, zatletic/stock.adobe.com.

Day 227: "Pope Francis has conducted the first canonisation of a married couple ...," Abaca Press/alamy.com.

Day 233: S. G. Rudl, *The Sermon on the Mount* (1928), Renáta Sedmáková/stock.adobe.com.

Day 235: Rembrandt, *St. Paul in Prison* (1627), restoredtraditions.com.